Expository
Sermons

Expository
Sermons

IAN R. K. PAISLEY

AMBASSADOR
Belfast • Greenville

Expository *Sermons*
Copyright © 1996 Ian R.K. Paisley

ISBN 1 898787 74 3

Published by

AMBASSADOR PRODUCTIONS, LTD.
Providence House
16 Hillview Avenue,
Belfast, BT5 6JR

Emerald House
1 Chick Springs Road, Suite 102
Greenville, South Carolina, 29609

Foreword

MY PREACHING IS BASED on the expositional method. I am a preacher of the Word. In spite of all opposition I announce my headings and seek to bring forth the sweetness, strength and sustenance from the passage which is before me. This is why the message retains its freshness for it is the pith and marrow, the cream and essence of the inbreathed Word of God. "Man cannot live but by every word of God is the truth which my Master has taught me."

In this volume the whole range of expositional preaching is demonstrated and illustrated from a text to a type, from the Decalogue to a Doctrine and finally to a whole Book.

The Bible is the inexhaustible Book. Its mines of gold have never been fully mined. I present in these sermons some of the treasures I have found therein.

Yours,
Set for the Defence
of the Gospel
Tan R. K. Paisley
Eph 6 : 19 + 20

February 1996
Martyrs Memorial Free Presbyterian Church,
356-376 Ravenhill Road,
Belfast, BT6 8GL
Northern Ireland

Contents

1 The greatest gathering
of all time

An exposition of Genesis 49:8-10 delivered to 4,000 people at the opening of the Fourth World Congress of Fundamentalists in the Founders Amphitorium on the Campus of Bob Jones University, Greenville, South Carolina, USA.

I CALL YOUR ATTENTION to Genesis, chapter 49, verses 9 to 12 - a death bed scene.

Ungodly men hate to contemplate death. Godly men love to contemplate death.

To the former, it is the door to darkness, doom and despair.

To the latter, it is the gateway to life, life more abundant and life indeed!

Herein is the difference between the other Gospel of the so-called Modernists and the Gospel of we Bible-defending Fundamentalists, who stand in true apostolic succession.

The perverted Gospel of modernism holds forth an *assignment* to men - it proclaims: "Behave like Christ and succeed."

The pure Gospel of Fundamentalism holds forth an *atonement* to men - It proclaims: "Believe on Christ and be saved."

The key to the first is *example by life*. The key to the second is *expiation by death*. The bloodshedding of Christ Crucified marks the great Divide. It is the Cross which makes them separate by an unbridgable gulf.

Death in Scripture then is vital to the Saints of God. This is one of the paradoxes of the Bible.

The first human death in Scripture was glorious. It was the death of the first Fundamentalist martyr, Abel - a victim of anti-Biblical unitarian Cainism. It was a death whose bloodshedding became a blood speaking. It spoke so loudly from the ground that God in the highest Heaven heard it.

The first human death recorded in the last book of the Bible is the death of yet another Fundamentalist martyr - Antipas (Rev. 2:13).

The supreme weapon of the devil - death - he is a murderer from the beginning - has been taken by God and has been transformed into the vehicle, not of our destruction but of our deliverance. Out of the womb of death has come forth the wonder of life. This is the mystery of the Cross and the demonstration of the wisdom and power of the Almighty.

O death, where is thy sting? Where? Where? Where? Search for it. Can you, dear child of God, find it?

O grave where is thy victory? Where? Where? Where? Seek it but you will never find it believing soul.

But you say, surely preacher, the sting of death is sin. I can find sin. Yes, but in the memory of God *forgiven sin* cannot be found.

Mel Trotter used to preach a great sermon on Isaiah, chapter 43, verse 25.

"I even I am He that blotteth out thy transgressions for Mine own sake, and will not remember thy sins."

He used the following outline. Our sins are all blotted out.

1..   **From God's Book.**
2.   **From God's Hand.**
3.   **For God's Sake.**
4.   **From God's Memory.**

But preacher does it not say the strength of sin is the law? Yes, but it also says, that Christ is the end of the law to everyone that believeth.

CH Spurgeon, as a boy preacher, had a great friend, an elderly preacher named Sutton. In Volume One of his autobiography Spurgeon records the following:

"Well, my dear sir, how are you?" was my salutation to him, one morning.

"I am pleased to see you so well at your age."

"Yes, I am in fine order for an old man and hardly feel myself failing at all."

"I hope your health will continue for years to come, and that, like Moses, you will go down to your grave with your eye undimmed and your natural force unabated."

"All very fine," said the old gentleman, "but, in the first place, Moses never went down to his grave at all, he went up to it; and in the next place, what is the meaning of all you have been talking about? Why did not the eye of Moses wax and dim?"

"I suppose sir," said I, very meekly, "that his natural mode of life and quiet spirit had helped to preserve his faculties and make him a vigorous old man."

"Very likely," he said, "but that's not what I'm driving at. What's the meaning, the spiritual teaching of the whole matter? Is it not just this? Moses is the law and what a glorious end of the law the Lord gave it on the Mount of His finished work; how sweetly its terrors were all laid to sleep with a kiss from God's mouth? And, mark you, the reason why the law no more condemns us is not because it's eye is dim, so that it cannot see our sins, or because of its force, with which to curse and punish us, is unabated; but Christ has taken the law up to the Mount and gloriously made and end of it."

But I digress. Of course I can plead apostolic example - going everywhere preaching the Word.

Here is a death bed scene. One of the strangest but sublimest in the whole history of the human race.

Jacob is not dying in the land of Promise, but in the foreign land of Egypt. He has come a long way from the day of his birth in the tent of his grandmother Sarah whom he never had the privilege of knowing.

J Wilbur Chapman, in his masterly sermon entitled: "A Broken Family Circle", described Jacob's pilgrimage thus:

"Through sunshine and storm he has come to the victorious end of a great life. By the way of deception practised upon his father, and deceit of which his brother was the object, also by the way of his passionate devotion to Rachel, until he claimed her as his own and by the way of the struggle at Jabbok's Ford, we find him reaching the place where he is a changed and chastened man, and limping out of weakness into power, he comes forth from the shadows into glorious light. His closing days are days of peace and the end of his journey is exceedingly beautiful."

Around the bed are his twelve sons - the sons of his four wives, Leah and her maid, Zilpah, Rachel and her maid, Bilhah.

'Tis a strange gathering of an even stranger family. The whole of the world's history is compressed here. The whole of redemption's history is condensed here. It is a holy place - the stage of history, the pulpit of prophecy and the room of mystery.

Look at those figures around the ancient patriarch - Reuben to Benjamin. It's the last time on earth Jacob will cast his eye upon them and call them by their names.

His staff, (the staff which was his only possession as he left his home at Rebecca's contrivance and Isaac's command, to seek a wife in his mother's family but really to escape the murderous wrath of his red-headed elder twin brother Esau), supports him as he utters one of the greatest prophecies in the whole Bible.

He uttered these, as Henry Law so pithily said: "When his eyes were closing to the speck of earth and opening to the expanse of heaven of boundless being."

Indeed the Heavenly glory, for a moment, overcame the earthly gloom and he saw and uttered things that only Heaven could reveal.

Note the three-foldness of its contents: (1) Compressed History; (2) Concentrated Prophecy; (3) Condensed Mystery.

I. COMPRESSED HISTORY

In these momentous words to the sons of Jacob we have traced the earthly history and Heavenly Glory of God's people.

In the first three sons we have a compressed history of our Depravity.

Like *Reuben* though possessing the highest natural position, the first born, we are (1) *Unstable* as water; (2) *Unable* to excel; and (3) *Unequalled* in sin. Did Reuben ever forget the dark sin of his adultery with one of his father's wives?

We need ever to remember the pit from which we have been digged and the rock from which we have been hewn.

In *Simeon* and *Levi* we have a compressed history of the totality of the depravity of our murder and rebellion in murdering the Son of God and rebelling against Him. The heart is deceitful above all things and desperately wicked, who can know it?

In *Judah* (with which we would especially concern ourselves at this Congress) we have a compressed history of the Coming of Christ and our gathering together unto Him. With Philip Doddridge we can say: "He drew me and I followed on, charmed to confess the voice divine.

In *Zebulin* and *Issachar* we have a compressed history of Service for Christ. We are saved to serve. Having got rid of the burden of our sin we should shoulder with joy the burden of His service.

In *Dan* we have a compressed history of Backsliding and Apostasy which has so spotted the history of Christianity. Note Dan does not make the roll call of the tribes in Revelation, chapter 7. His name is missing. His tribe supplies not one of the elect, the sealed ones, the chosen of God.

In *Gad* - meaning Victory at the end - *Asher* meaning Blessed and *Naphtali* meaning Freedom and Worship, we have a compressed history of the Trials, Temptations, Testings, Tribulations and Triumphs of the Remnant Testimony amidst Apostasy.

In *Joseph* we have a compressed history of the Reigning and Coming of Christ. His bow abides in Strength

In *Benjamin* we have a compressed history of both our millennial and perennial reign with Him, when we will enter fully into being sons of His right hand.

It is to be noted that on the high priest's garment *Reuben*, the first of the twelve, is represented by the *jasper* stone and *Benjamin*, the last of the twelve, by a *sardine* stone. In Revelation, chapter 4, verse 3, mark carefully the vision of God is compared to these two stones.

"And he that sat was to look upon like a jasper and a sardine stone and there was a rainbow round about the throne, in sight like unto an emerald."

For God in all history *past, present and future* folds all eternity, and ever present now, unfolds.

But the contents of Jacob's farewell is not only a Condensed History, it is also a Concentrated Prophecy.

II. CONCENTRATED PROPHECY

The whole chapter is prophecy in concentrate.

Ever keep in mind the Bible definition of prophecy: "the testimony of Jesus is the Spirit of Prophecy," Revelation 19:10.

Touch the chapter anywhere and you touch Christ somewhere. Oh to have eyes to see Him and hearts to receive Him.

In the first five Books of Moses we have seven prophetic representations of Christ. Seven is the perfect number so it is a perfect prophetic representation of Christ.

1.   Seed: Genesis 3:15
2.   Shiloh: Genesis 49:10*

3.   Shepherd: Genesis 49:24*
4.   Stone: Genesis 49:24*
5.   Staff: Numbers 18:8
6.   Star: Numbers 24:17
7.   Sceptre: Numbers 24:17

Notice three out of the seven occur in this chapter with the one "Shiloh" in the particular part of the chapter we have under study.

In any scripture seven the divine order is important. The fourth stands for the centre. The fourth here in these seven prophetic representations of Christ is the *Stone*. How appropriate that is. The Stone is underscored. It has reference to the glorious resurrection of our Lord Jesus and the centrality of His person in the structure of His Church. "The Stone which the builders refused is become the head stone of the corner. This is the Lord's doing and is marvellous in our eyes," Psalm 118:22 and 23; Matthew 21:42; Mark 12:10 and 11; Luke 20:17; Acts 4:11; I Peter 2:4.

Now the third and the fifth are always linked in any scripture seven. It's not hard to see the connection here. The third is the *Shepherd* and the fifth is the *Staff*. The second and the sixth go together. The *Shiloh* is the second and the *Star* is the sixth. We will see how closely those are connected. The first and the seventh go together. The *Seed* is the first and the *Sceptre* is the seventh. The bruised seed gained the burnished sceptre, for by His bruised heel He crushed the serpent's head forever.

This is but an example of the Concentrated Prophecy in the chapter.

But the contents of Jacob's farewell is not only Compressed History and concentrated Prophecy, it is also Condensed Mystery. It is into that mystery we want to look as we come to ponder the phrase "Unto Him shall the gathering of the people be."

III. CONDENSED MYSTERY

The mysteries of scripture are not hidden mysteries but are always, to the believer, revealed mysteries. Therefore the mystery can be unlocked out of the Word. Oh to behold the wonder of all wonders, our Blessed Lord Himself.

Having briefly sketched in the background let me now come to my allotted subject. "The Summons to the Gathering."

A casual look at Jacob's blessing of his son Judah can be seen to be in a threefold setting with Judah's name called three times. (10 of Jacob's sons are named but once. Joseph is named twice while Judah is named three times.) Verse 8 ... First part. Verse 9 ... Second part. Verses 10, 11 and 12 ... Third part.

If we are to rightly understand the Summons, we must with care consider from whence it comes.

Oh for the illumination of the Holy Spirit! For He who wrote the Book can best expound what He Himself wrote.

Without a doubt a greater than Judah is here, even He who came to Judah's tribe to be the Saviour of the race.

Looking at these three condensed mysteries of Christ, I would adopt the scriptural principle, the last shall be first, and look first at verses 10, 11 and 12.

FIRSTLY: THE SUMMONS FROM THE CROSS

Now the Cross is the place of outpoured blood and the blood is the life. Therefore the value of the blood is the value of the life. The efficacy of the Passion is measured by the efficacy of the Person. The whole life of the God-man flows in crimson liquidity from the old tree of Calvary.

It is no wonder these verses give us the Holy Spirit's thumbnail biography of the life of Christ culminating in the Cross.

"Unto Shiloh come?" Mark those words carefully. Who is Shiloh? Most clearly He is the promised seed of the woman.

We must carefully distinguish between the tribal aspects of this prophecy and the differences between these and the Kingdom aspects. The political aspects relate to the tribes, the spiritual aspects relate to the Kingdom.

The Hebrew word translated "sceptre" is a word for the tribe and in verse twenty-eight it is so translated. "The twelve tribes of Israel."

You see the political sceptre did depart from Judah again and again but the tribal sceptre never.

Munro Gibson states:

"When we bear this in mind, instead of encountering serious difficulty, as those do who understand the sceptre to be the symbol of royalty here, from the fact that again and again the political sceptre did depart from Judah; we recognise a very striking correspondence with the facts of history. Before Shiloh came, all other tribes had been blotted from the map of Palestine. There in Galilee on the north, Samaria in the centre and Peraea in the east - covering the territory that belonged to the ten tribes of the northern kingdom; and in the south, little Benjamin and the remnant of Simeon, long before scattered Israel, according to Jacob's prophecy, are now merged in JUDEA, the historical representative of the old, and now the only separately surviving tribe of Judah."

"SHILOH"

There have been many interpretations put forward concerning the meaning of this word but the majority view (which I believe is the right view) is that Shiloh belongs to that Shalom family of Hebrew words meaning peace or rest and means the One who brings peace - the One who gives rest.

This interpretation agrees completely with the first use of the name for the place where the Tabernacle was erected in the land of promise after God had given rest from the enemies of Israel.

In I Chronicles 5:2 we see the setting aside of Reuben, the first born of Leah, and Joseph, the first born of Rachel, and we read: For Judah prevailed above his brethren and of him came the Chief Ruler."

When this is compared with the title of the Chief Ruler revealed by Isaiah the full meaning of Shiloh is seen. Isaiah 9:6: "For unto us a Child is born, unto us a Son is given: and the government shall be upon His shoulder: and His name shall be called Wonderful, Counsellor, The mighty God, the everlasting Father, The Prince of Peace." - The Prince of Peace. Shiloh.

The name Solomon in the Hebrew is closely similar to Shiloh.

When we looked briefly in our introduction at the seven prophetic representations of Christ in the Pentateuch I asked you to note that Shiloh in this prophecy of Jacob was related to the Star of the prophecy of Baalim. Numbers 24:17.

So excited were the angels of God at the Birth of the Son of God that they burst through the bounds of invisibility in their thousands and cried: "Glory to God in the highest and on earth, peace, goodwill toward men." Luke 2:14.

Now note that the name Judah means praise of God (Genesis 29:35) - "glory to God" and Shiloh means "peace".

If the angels spoke in the Hebrew tongue then they would have used the two words *Judah* in the highest and on earth *Shiloh,* peace goodwill. Emmanuel had come, God with us.

From verse 10 we turn to verse 11 and we approach the Cross. For His Birth was in order to His Bleeding and His Cribbing in order to His Crucifying.

We are reminded of His triumphal entry into Jerusalem. Here centuries beforehand that entry was prophetically put in its right context - its relation to the Cross.

Compare this scripture and its reference to the foal and ass's colt in Zechariah's prophecy, chapter 9:9 and 10 and the part of fulfilment in Matthew 21:4 and 5. Note carefully it is but a part of fulfilment. If you want an interesting and instructive study of this I recommend Sir Robert Anderson's *The Coming Prince*.

The Lord Jesus is hastening up to Jerusalem. His hour is come. Mark 10:32-34.

"And they were in the way going up to Jerusalem; and Jesus went before them; and they were amazed; and as they followed, they were afraid. And He took again the twelve, and began to tell them what things should happen unto Him.

Saying: Behold, we go up to Jerusalem; and the son of Man shall be delivered unto the chief priests and unto the scribes; and they shall condemn Him unto death, and shall deliver Him to the Gentiles:

And the shall mock Him and shall scourge Him and shall spit upon Him and shall kill Him: and the third day he shall rise again."

See the disciples hold back. They are afraid. Not so our Lord. Notice how He hastened on before them and they, but reluctant followers, behind.

In order to hasten His arrival at Jerusalem He sends for the ass and the colt of the ass. He rides forward to the place of His death. What is He doing? He is fulfilling what Jacob on his death bed saw would happen in the last days. He binds His foal to the vine and the ass's colt to the choicest vine for He Himself is that true vine from which the wine - the blood of the grape shall flow.

Note carefully Luke's account and once again we have Shiloh mentioned. At His wondrous birth as we have already seen, residents from Heaven cried: "Peace = Shiloh on Earth." Now in His triumphant entry men and women cry out: "Peace = Shiloh in Heaven." The object of His death is making peace for us in Heaven and then applying the fruits of that peace in our hearts on earth. Shiloh in heaven and Shiloh on earth. Hosannah to His Name for evermore.

"He washed His garments in wine and His clothes in the blood of grapes," verse 11. Those words bring to our mind immediately Isaiah 63:1-4.

"Who is this that cometh from Edom, with dried garments from Bozrah? this that is glorious in his apparel, travelling in the greatness of his strength? I that speak in righteousness, mighty to save.

Wherefore art thou red in thine apparel, and thy garments like him that treadeth in the winefat?

I have trodden the winepress alone; and of the people there was none with me: for I will tread them in mine anger, and trample them in my fury; and their blood shall be sprinkled upon my garments, and I will stain all my raiment. For the day of vengeance is in mine heart, and the year of my redeemed is come."

Here is the *Struggle* of the Cross.

"His eyes shall be red with wine." What a thought is here. The eyes of Jesus filled with blood. The Crown of thorns sent streams of blood down the forehead of my Beloved. The blood literally filled His eyes. His eyes were red with wine. Jacob saw it by faith. It was not yet fulfilled. Herein is the *Suffering* of the Cross.

"His teeth white with milk." Ah, here we have the sincere milk of the Word. How sweet were those seven words He uttered on the tree. Yes, and His words had a bite. His teeth are white with milk. Herein we have the *Summons* of the Cross.

Brethren it is from the Cross and to the Cross that the Summons comes.

In that summons is an awful mixture - the crack of the Roman scourge and the consequent lash on Christ's back - the tearing of the hair from off the Saviour's face - the driving of the thorns into His brow as He is struck on the thorn-crowned head with a reed - buffeting and beating in Pilate's judgment hall by one hundred brutal soldiers of Caesar's army and Pilate's guard and their spitting on the very face of the Son of God.

In that summons is the terrifying concentration of the barbarism of crucifixion - the stripping naked of the victim, the nailing of hands and feet to the tree, the pulling out of every bone and joint as the butt of the stake is put into a crevice in the rocks. And all accompanied with the trickling blood from hands, feet, brow, and back, each trickle joining the other to make a fountain at the Cross's foot.

In that summons is the fearsome condensing of the three hours of darkness when Christ went into the very eye of God's awful storm of wrath upon sin - when He endured such affliction that had He not been Omnipotent He would have died the victim and not the victor - the agony which brought from the heart of the Sufferer that mysterious cry, "My God, My God, why hast Thou forsaken me!"

In that summons is the unparalleled compression of an energy which marks the summit of Divine Almightiness. What dying man in the last moment could cry with a loud voice such a message - FINISHED - a cry which brought about earthquakes, resurrections and the tearing in twain of the great temple veil which divided the Holiest of All from the Holy Places.

Are our ears so heavy - so waxed over with carnal indifference, worldly lusts, and denominational pride that we do not hear - nay cannot hear this summons mingled in this awful mixture, this terrifying concentration, this fearsome condensation and this unparalleled compression.

By His death and bloody Passion, to quote the old litany, I demand this day a hearing for my Lord and Master Jesus Christ.

SECONDLY: THE SUMMONS FROM THE THRONE

"Judah is a lion's whelp: from the prey, my son, thou art gone up: he stooped down, he couched as a lion, and as an old lion; who shall rouse him up!" Genesis 49:9

It can be seen from these words that the Summons *secondly is The Summons from the Throne.*

This verse from the first book of the Bible can be best expounded in the light of the last book of the Bible.

Have you ever noticed that in the Book of Revelation you have a parade of evil beasts, the great red dragon that old serpent the devil, chapters 2 and 20, the beast with the characteristics of leopard, bear and lion and again in Chapters 13 and 17, the beast with two horns like a lamb but with speech of a dragon; chapter 13.

However, before any of these beasts appear, we are given the unveiling of another beast greater and stronger than them all.

John is in tears. The mysterious Book of God is unopened and unread. No man in Heaven and earth or under the earth is worthy or able to open or read the Divine Volume. Revelation 5:5 and 6.

"And one of the elders saith unto me, Weep not: behold, the Lion of the tribe of Juda, the Root of David, hath prevailed to open the Book, and to loose the seven seals thereof.

And I beheld, and, lo, in the midst of the throne and of the four beasts and in the midst of the elders, stood a Lamb as it had been slain, having seven horns and seven eyes, which are the seven spirits of God sent forth into all the earth.

Note it well, the Lion of Judah's tribe.

Genesis 49:9.

"Judah is a lion's whelp: from the prey, my son, thou art gone up: he stooped down, he couched as a lion, and as an old lion, who shall rouse him up!"

Herein is the life story of the lion. First in youth - the whelp. Second in battle - the lion and third, in triumph - the old lion.

This thought of the lion reappears in the Messianic prophecy.

Notice the parallelism in Baalim's prophecy. The three stages of the lion's life are mentioned yet again.

Numbers 23:24, Numbers 24:9.

"Behold, the people shall rise up as a great lion, and lift up himself as a young lion: he shall not lie down until he eat of the prey and drink of the slain."

"He couched, he lay down as a lion, and as a great lion: who shall stir him up? Blessed is he that blesseth thee, and cursed is he that curseth thee."

Christ is seen as a lion's whelp when His first recorded words are noted in the Gospel of Luke. Luke, chapter 2:46-50.

"And it came to pass, that after three days they found Him in the temple sitting in the midst of the doctors, both hearing them and asking questions.

And all that heard Him were astonished at His understanding and answers.

And when they saw Him, they were amazed: and His mother said unto Him, Son, why hast Thou thus dealt with us? behold Thy father and I have sought Thee sorrowing.

And He said unto them: How is it that ye sought Me? Wist ye not that I must be about my Father's business."

Those questions were significant and His answer to Mary even more so. The whole of His energy was bent about His Father's business. There was no loss of that strength for when he had completed His Father's business He cried with *a loud voice,* "It is finished."

As a mature lion He took the prey at the Cross dividing the spoil with the strong (Isaiah 53) and receiving gifts for men (Psalm 68).

As an old lion He occupies the Eternal Throne. The Lion of Judah's tribe!

Behold Him! And as John looked to see the Lion he saw instead the Lamb. The One to whom John the Baptist pointed to in John 1:29.

But a miracle was manifested. The lamb was newly slain. Its blood was shed yet it *stood in* triumph. It reclined not in death but rather reigned in life.

The lion's whelp - the mature lion - the old lion are one and the same as the Lamb and that Lamb is all the glory in Emmanuel's Land.

He is in the midst of the Throne. The Summons brethren is from the Throne. We're under marching orders from the King.

The Summons comes to us mingled with the glorious harmony of the new song, the glad shouts of the innumerable elect angels and the united Hosannahs of all creation.

It is a Throne Summons. We dare not, must not refuse it. Ours is to obey. We must work from the Throne and to the Throne. To wear the livery of the King of Kings and be employed in His blessed Service is heaven begun below.

THIRDLY: THE SUMMONS FROM THE TEMPLE

And now thirdly and finally we come to verse 8:

"Judah thou art he who thy brethren shall praise: Thy hand shall be in the neck of Thine enemies; Thy Father's children shall bow down before thee." (verse 8).

The Summons is not only from the Cross and from the Throne but it is also from the Temple.

What a temple this is, in which in all things He, our Lord Jesus Christ, doth have the pre-eminence.

The temple of the Lord is characterised by three things.

Firstly, The Song: "Thou are He whom Thy brethren shall praise.

The brethren of Christ, those born into His family, have a song and it is a Song of Praise of and to their Beloved

His Name is above every name
His Work is above every work
His Blessing is above every blessing
His Victory is above every victory.

To Him alone the praise shall be given. This is no party song. Alas today many have been taken up with the party and have forsaken the person.

We worship not at the golden calf of the denominational shrine. We have not come to burn incense at the altar of organised fundamentalism. Nay rather we have come to give all the honour, all the praise and all the glory to the Sole King and Only head of the Church, Our Lord Jesus Christ. Every other so-called head is a deceiver and an imposter. Unto Him, Unto Him, Unto Him alone shall the gathering of the people be.

Jesus, Blessed Jesus, Thou art He whom Thy brethren shall praise.

The temple is secondly characterised by *The Sovereign:* "Thy hand shall be in the neck of Thine enemies."

This sovereignty is not one of judgment but one of mercy. The act in Scripture of putting one's feet on the neck of the enemy was a sovereign act of total judgment. See Joshua 10:24.

The act of putting the hand on the enemies neck was one of forgiveness and mercy and blessing. Isaac felt the neck of Jacob. Thank God, we who were enemies, He has reconciled unto God. We have felt His nail pierced hand upon our necks and like John we have heard the sweetest of all words, "Fear not."

The temple is thirdly characterised by *Births and Worship:* "Thy Father's children shall bow down before thee."

The shouts of new born babes and their worship shows that Christ in His temple shall see His seed.

We have a preview of this in the gospel. Matthew 21:15-16.

"And when the chief priests and scribes saw the wonderful things and the children crying in the temple, and saying, Hosannah to the Son of David: they were sore displeased. And said unto Him, Hearest Thou what these say? And Jesus saith unto them, Yea: have ye never read, Out of the mouths of babes and sucklings thou hast perfected praise."

The Summons from the Temple. It comes mingled with the praises of the brethren, the sovereignty of Divine pardon and the cries of the new born souls. How can we shut our ears to such a summons? "He that hath ears to hear let him hear."

Those words were never used nor could be used by mortal man. They came firstly and finally in the Holy Scripture from the lips of God incarnate in the flesh, from the One who Himself alone boasts the title, Word of God.

Seven times and seven times only is it recorded that while the Lord Jesus tabernacled among men He used these words.

Seven is of course the number of perfection. Note how they are all related with the Word of God in its different aspects.

Their first speaking Luke 8:8 was after Our Lord first told the parable of the Sower and before the appointment of the twelve to go on their preaching mission. See Luke 9:2.

The second speaking, Matthew 11:15, in reference to the preaching ministry of the forerunner John the Baptist and his person and place.

Their third speaking was after the appointment of preaching the mission of the twelve, Matthew 11:1 and our Lord gave the parable of the Sower the second time in Matthew 13:9, the first parable in a series of seven.

Their fourth speaking is after the explanation of the parable of the tares in Matthew 13:43.

The fourth in any scripture seven is the great centre - so hence the importance of this parable. It sums up the whole situation of our day. Compare Matthew 13: 24-30 and verses 36-43.

Their fifth speaking was in Mark 7:16 after He had explained the source of man's defilement.

The seventh speaking was in Luke 14:35 after He had set out the salt of the Word in the cost of discipleship.

The Glorified Christ in Heaven again spoke these words through His Holy Spirit to His people on earth when from the Throne He addressed the seven Churches which were in Asia.

Revelation, Chapter 2, verses 7, 11, 17, 29. Chapter 3, verses 6, 13 and 22. I bid you compare these seven with the seven in the Gospels. They are parallel. Their final use is in the culminating battle with the beast, Revelation 13, verses 7-9. I wonder have you the hearing ear for the Summons - from the Cross - from the Throne - from the Temple.

If the Lord tarries, one day each servant will receive that Summons to the Father's House.

I cannot do better than repeat the description given in Bunyan's classic, The Pilgrim's Progress, of the summonsing of Mr Valiant-for-Truth to receive his award.

"After this, it was noised abroad, that Mr Valiant-for-Truth was taken with a summons by the same post as the other; and had this for a token that the summons was true, that his pitcher was broken at the fountain. When he understood it, he called for his friends and told them of it. Then, he said, I am going to my Father's and tho' with great difficulty I am got hither, yet now I do not repent me of all the trouble I have been at to arrive where I am. My Sword I give to him that shall succeed me in my Pilgrimage, and my Courage and Skill to him that can get it. My marks and scars I carry with me, to be a witness for me, that I have fought His battles, who now will be my Rewarder. When the day that he must go hence was come, many accompany'd him to the River-side, into which he went, he said,

Death, where is thy Sting? And as he went down deeper, he said, Grave, where is thy Victory? So he passed over, and all the Trumpets sounded for him on the other side."

How aptly do these words apply to those whom we knew our departed brethren in Christ, the stalwarts of Fundamentalism. Men like the founder of this great school, Dr Bob Jones, Snr., my own beloved father and a great galaxy of others including Dr Ward Ayer and Dr Eastep. But the greatest of all the summons will be to that great meeting in the air when our Lord shall come again.

Behold the archangel of God. He waits patiently to blow the trumpet blast which will mark the climax of the ages. His celestial lips quiver in delightful expectation of the happening which will be triggered at the sounding of the last trump.

What a summons that will be. The redeemed of all ages who have died and whose remains have occupied some place in this universe - in the dust of the earth, in the briny sea or the elements of the atmosphere - will all rise again. The dead in Christ shall rise first. The saints still living will be changed and together, on that blessed togetherness, all disunity gone forever - we will be caught up to meet the Lord in the air - so shall we ever be with the Lord. Unto *Him* shall the gathering of the people be. Blessed is he that is called to the Marriage Supper of the Lamb.

ADVENT

The Church has waited long,
Her absent Lord to see;
And still in loneliness she waits,
A friendless stranger she.
Age after age has gone,
Sun after sun has set,
And still, in weeds of widowhood,
She weeps a mourner yet.
Come, then, Lord Jesus, come!

Saint after saint on earth,
has lived and loved and died;
And as they left us one by one,
We laid them side by side;

We laid them down to sleep,
But not in hope forlorn,
We laid them but to ripen there,
Till the last glorious morn.
Come, then, Lord Jesus, come!

The serpent's brood increased,
The powers of hell grow bold,
The conflict thickens, faith is low,
And love is waxing cold.
How long, O Lord our God,
Holy and true and good,
Wilt thou not judge thy suffering Church,
Her sighs and tears and blood?
Come, then, Lord Jesus, come.

We long to hear Thy voice,
To see Thee face to face,
To share Thy crown and glory then,
As now we share Thy grace.
Should not the loving bride
The absent bridegroom mourn?
Should she not wear the weeds of grief
Until her Lord return?
Come, then, Lord Jesus, come.

The whole creation groans,
And waits to hear that voice,
That shall restore her comeliness,
And make her wastes rejoice.
Come, Lord, and wipe away,
The curse, the sin, the stain,
And make this blighted world of ours
Thine Own fair world again.
Come, then, Lord Jesus, come!

~ Horatius Bonar

Have you the hearing ear? Sinner hear and you shall be redeemed. Backslider hear and you shall be restored. Saint hear and you shall be revived. Harken the Summons is to you.

Amen and Amen

2 A look at *Luke's book*

A SERIES OF FOUR SERMONS ON THE GOSPEL OF LUKE, PREACHED IN THE MARTYRS MEMORIAL CHURCH, BELFAST AND FIRST PRINTED IN 1973. THE SUBJECTS ARE: LUKE'S GOSPEL - A CHRONICLE OF PRAYER, LUKE'S GOSPEL - A COMPILATION OF PRAISE, LUKE'S GOSPEL - A COMPENDIUM OF POWER AND LUKE'S GOSPEL - A COMPANION OF PILGRIMAGE.

ONE
LUKE'S GOSPEL - A CHRONICLE OF PRAYER

I WANT YOU TO OPEN your Bible with me at the Gospel according to Luke. I want to commence a series of four messages entitled "A Look at Luke's Book."

THE SAME BUT DIFFERENT

Could I say that every book of the Bible is absolutely the same, yet absolutely different. It is absolutely the same because it has the same great theme. The theme of every book of the Bible, if we had eyes to perceive it, is the Lord Jesus Christ. Each book of the Bible is however, absolutely different because the viewpoint that is taken of the Lord Jesus Christ in each book of the Bible is entirely and uniquely different.

Oh yes, there is only one Christ; one wonderful life of that one wonderful sacrifice of that one wonderful Christ. Yet we have four gospels all relating, from a different viewpoint, to that one wonderful life of the Saviour.

THE FORESHADOWING OF THE FOUR GOSPELS IN GENESIS

Of course, there are suggestions in the Old Testament that there would be four gospels. Turn over to the book of Genesis and in the book of Genesis you will find the story of the planting of a garden in Eden. In chapter two of Genesis there is the garden and there is the world. In the garden there is the tree of life. Now all God's dwelling places depicted in the Bible have three special compartments. In the tabernacle you have the outer court. In the tabernacle you have the holy place. In the tabernacle you have the holiest of all. Now in God's first dwelling place with man there was the outer world, there was the garden of Eden and there was the tree of life. The outer world corresponds to the outer court of the tabernacle. The garden of Eden corresponds to the holy place. The tree of life corresponds to the holiest of all.

Now in this garden there was a river. One river! There is but one Christ. One Christ to satisfy a world of thirsty souls. One Christ Who is the Bread of Life to hungry men. One Christ Who is the one Saviour of a lost and ruined and accursed race. The river parts into four heads. The river of Christ's life parts into four biographies, four life stories. You will notice that in the first one the emphasis is upon the King. You can work out the others for yourself.

THE FOUR GOSPELS IN EXODUS

Could I say then, when we come over to Exodus we have this suggested to us again. Turn over to Exodus chapter thirty, and there you will find there was special oil. That oil was for the anointing of the priests. The Lord Jesus Christ was anointed with the oil of gladness above His fellows. It was that anointing which resulted in His wonderful life here on earth. But if you look at the make-up of that oil in Exodus chapter thirty and verse twenty-three, you will find that it had four principal spices.

Four! Myrrh, cinnamon, sweet calamus and cassia. Four principal spices! Now if you take great care in meditation you will also discover that these four spices represent the four gospels. Perhaps we have a little hint of that in Matthew when they presented unto Him gold, frankincense and myrrh. And myrrh is the first spice that is suggested here in Exodus thirty.

Of course, man did not write the Bible, He would not have known anything about it. If you had been writing the Bible, you could not have put them in any order. It would not have mattered for you would not have known their meaning or their significance. The order in scripture however is entirely and absolutely correct.

THE FOUR GOSPELS IN EZEKIEL

We turn over to the book of Ezekiel and we find there the representation of the four gospels again. There is the face of a man, the face of a lion, the face of an ox and the face of an eagle, Ezekiel chapter one and verse ten. These four faces represent the four gospels. The Lord Jesus Christ is seen as the lion. He is seen as the ox. He is seen as the man. He is seen as the flying eagle. The lion, the king of the beasts, is known for its majesty. You will see Christ in His majesty in Matthew for Matthew is the gospel of the Sovereign. In Matthew Jesus Christ meets the Jew. So in Matthew He is the Son of David the King, and the Son of Abraham, the father of the nation.

In Mark's gospel there is no reference whatever to His birth. Why? Because Mark is the gospel of the Servant, not of the Son. Nobody wants to know the genealogy of the servant. The servant is the worker. No one is interested in who his father or mother were. All they are interested in is "Can he do the job?" In Marks' gospel He is the Servant. The ox that labours for God!

In Luke's gospel He is traced back to Adam in His genealogy. In Luke's gospel He is the Son of man. He is the Son of man. His genealogy goes back to Adam. We have Him as the face of a man.

And then in John's gospel you see Him as the Son of God. The flying eagle is the bird which masters the heavens. You see Him as the master of the heavens in John. The eternal Word, Who, in the beginning, was with God and was God.

THE UNIQUENESS OF LUKE'S GOSPEL

So we have learned that Matthew is the gospel of the Sovereign. Mark is the gospel of the servant. Luke is the gospel of the Saviour and John is the gospel of the Son. In keeping with that, moreover, the gospel of Luke is completely and entirely unique. It is a unique gospel! I will tell you why. In Luke's gospel the sympathetic man, a man surrounded by people. There are more crowds in Luke's gospel than in any other gospel. He is more with the people in Luke's gospel than in any other gospel. He is more in those resorts where men gather because He is the sympathetic man. He is the glorious Saviour of men. Of course, it is also unique that Luke was the writer, because Luke was the beloved physician, and He was a sympathetic man himself in his own sphere.

He was the companion of the Apostle Paul. If you check in Colossians chapter four you have the suggestion that he was a Gentile, the only Gentile who wrote any book of the Bible. The gospel of Christ jumps national barriers and cuts across the colours of men and the classes of their nations. It is one Christ for the whole world. Luke emphasises Christ as the Saviour of all men, but especially of them that believe, as the inspired scripture puts it so well.

LUKE'S GOSPEL IS A CHRONICLE OF PRAYER

The first thing I want to show you about Luke's gospel which is completely unique is that it is a chronicle of prayer! You want to be God's man? You want to be God's woman? You need to pray. You need to learn the secret of prayer. You need to know the power of prayer. You need to experience the deliverances of prayer.

CHRIST BORN IN ANSWER TO AN OLD WOMAN'S PRAYER

You know the unique thing about Luke's gospel is this, that according to Luke's gospel, Jesus Christ was born in answer to the prayers of an old woman of eighty-four years of age. So the prayers of an elderly woman are very important!

Turn over to chapter one of Luke's gospel, and you will find there the story of the birth of John, and then you have the story of the birth of the Lord Jesus. In chapter two you have the story of the Lord Jesus carried into the temple. We come to verse thirty-six: "And there was one Anna, a prophetess, the daughter of Phanuel, of the tribe of Aser: she was of a great age, and had lived with an husband seven years from her virginity; and she was a widow of about four-score and four years, which departed not from the temple, but served God with fastings and prayers night and day. And she coming in that instant gave thanks likewise unto the Lord, and spake of Him to all them that looked for redemption in Jerusalem." She was spending her days praying for Jesus to come, and Jesus came as a result of an old woman's prayers. Could there be anything that honours prayer more than that and elevates prayer more than that, emphasises prayer more than that, and underscores the importance, the power, and the effectiveness of prayer more than that?

What is more, Luke is the gospel writer who tells you of times when Jesus prayed, when no other writer tells you that he was praying.

CHRIST PRAYED AT HIS BAPTISM

The Lord Jesus Christ commenced His public ministry at His baptism by John in Jordan. That was the first time He was shown publicly to the people. Chapter three and verse twenty one says: "Now when all the people were baptised, it came to pass, that Jesus also being baptised, and praying." The first time that the Lord Jesus was seen at the commencement of His public ministry, He was seen in the act of prayer. This is in keeping with Luke's gospel, because I told you that Luke's gospel brings out the fact that Jesus Christ is the sympathetic man, that Jesus Christ is the Saviour of the world. The first time the world sees Him in public, it sees Him in the act of intercession. Yes and, praise God, as I peer into the heavens, Jesus is still praying for us. He still carries on His great intercessory work as our glorified High Priest on the Father's Throne. It is good to know that Jesus is praying for us.

CHRIST TOOK TIME TO PRAY

Turn over to chapter five and verse sixteen. And here in this chapter you have the story of His miracles. He is showing forth His power. He is cleansing the leper. Verse fifteen: "But so much the more went there a fame abroad of him: and great multitudes came together to hear, and to be healed by Him of their infirmities." Here you have the great multitudes and the crowds pressing in upon Him. The unceasing throngs gathered to hear His words, and to see and experience His power to heal. And then Luke says in verse sixteen, "And He withdrew Himself into the wilderness, and prayed." Underline it! Amidst all the bustle, amidst all the throng, amidst all the calls for His ministry and His healing touch He withdrew to the wilderness. Away from the throng, and away from the crowd, away from the bustle and away from the multitudes, my Blessed Lord kneeled down to pray. Would to God His people would follow that example. Would to God, amidst the bustle of this old world, and amidst the calls upon God's people for their ministry and their service, that we would learn the blessed secret of which our Lord sets us so gracious and so wonderful an example in Luke's gospel: "And He prayed."

CHRIST PRAYED ALL NIGHT

Let us turn over to the sixth chapter. Here we have the Lord Jesus Christ facing the religious leaders of His day in great controversy. They were mere traditionalists emphasising the letter of the law, and rejecting the spirit of it. Now after His controversy with these traditionalists, and these that rejected the spirit of the law we read "And they were filled with madness; and communed one with another what they might do to Jesus." Verse 11. What does the Lord do? The Lord Jesus in the midst of the tempest of this ferocious controversy that is brought down upon His head by the traditionalists of His days retired to pray. Verse 12: "And it came to pass in those days, that He went out into a mountain to pray, and continued all night in prayer to God.

So when the battle is at its hottest, when the conflict is raging in all its fiercest intensity, when the confrontation with the powers of darkness is upon us, and when we are in the throes of tremendous assaults from the enemy, we have to learn the secret to get alone with God. In the night seasons when men sleep, we must learn to supplicate. And in a day when men have forgotten to pray, we have to be in the business of zealous intercession before God. He has shown us an example that we should follow in His steps.

CHRIST PRAYED ALONE

Turn over to the ninth chapter and in this ninth chapter you will find that the Lord Jesus Christ again is in prayer. He has fed the five thousand. He has wrought the great miracle. But immediately after that tremendous miracle of feeding the five thousand, He goes away alone. Verse eighteen of chapter nine: "And it came to pass, as He was alone praying." Alone!

It is good to pray with our brethren. It is good to pray with the people of God. But there is a time when we must go it alone. "The Father that seeth in secret shall reward thee openly." "When thou prayest, do not stand at the end of the street, do not be like the pharisees, but enter into thy closet, and shut to the door, and there pray." The scripture teaches us here of the Blessed Man of Luke's gospel, "He was alone praying."

CHRIST PRAYED IN HIS TRANSFIGURATION

Let us turn over in the same chapter, and let us come down to verse twenty eight. Here we find prayer related to His transfiguration "He took Peter and John and James, and went into a mountain to pray. (verse twenty eight). And as He prayed, the fashion of His countenance was altered, and His raiment was white and glistening." I see those apostles probably sitting around Him as He prayed, and suddenly His countenance is changed, and in the midst of His prayer, the glory of His Deity bursts forth and lights up His whole manhood, and He communes with men in the glory land.

I am telling you my brother and sister, if you learn to pray, your prayer room will become a mount of transfiguration to you. If you learn how to pray the way you ought to pray, you will be changed as you kneel at the throne of grace, and you will enjoy heavenly communion with the glory land. You will commune through the Word with that great company that no man can number. For God says, "Seeing we are compassed about with so great a cloud of witnesses," the onlookers from the glory land., the men and women who walked this path before us, praise God, are looking on at us now. The transfiguration mountain was a mountain of prayer!

THE DISCIPLES WANTED TO PRAY LIKE JESUS

Turn to the eleventh chapter and verse one: "And it came to pass, that as He was praying in a certain place, when He ceased, one of His disciples said unto Him, Lord, teach us to pray." That is a very intriguing passage you know. His disciples are gathered around Him, and the Lord is praying. And when they heard Him pray, they learned that they never really prayed. They learned how hopeless and how poor were their prayers.

When I consider my great intercessor, I hang my head in shame. How weak, how impotent, how poor are my prayers and my prayer life!

The disciples were so fascinated with our Lord in prayer, that immediately He finished His prayer what did they say? "Lord, teach us to pray the way you pray."

The Lord wondered that there was no intercessor. The Lord is looking for men and women who can stand in the gap and can pray. I tell you, you will learn to pray if you keep in the company of the Lord Jesus, because He is the great Man of prayer, the sympathetic Man. We have here the disciples' prayer, wrongly called the Lord's Prayer.

It is the disciples' prayer and it is the basis for all praying. Some day we will consider it in all its wonderful significance.

THE INDIVIDUALITY OF CHRIST'S PRAYERS

Let us turn to the twenty second chapter of Luke, and verse thirty one: "And the Lord said, Simon, Simon, behold, Satan hath desireth to have you, that he may sift you as wheat: But I have prayed for thee, that thy faith fail not." "I have prayed for thee."

We learn here the individuality of Christ's prayers. Do you know friend that Christ prays for you? Do you know that? Mother, amidst the cares and the crosses of your life, keeping the home tidy and clean, preparing the clothes for your family and the food for the festal board, doing the insignificant things that no one really knows you do every day and there is no discharge from your duties, and there is no rest from your cares. Jesus says: "I have prayed for thee." Jesus understands! Is that not a great thing?

Father, out there at the bench, winning the bread among the workmates and amidst the toil and heat of the day, when no one cares, except your nearest and dearest, and no one understands, Jesus understands and He prays for you.

Is it not good to know that Jesus prays for us individually. He says: "I have prayed for thee, that thy faith fail not." I want to tell you something. Every prayer Jesus offers is answered. Do you know that? He says: "I know Father Thou hearest me always." If you study prayer in the Bible, you will find if God hears your prayer, He answers it. Once you get the ear of God, you have got the answer. You have to labour until God hears you. Once God hears you, you can close up and go home. It is all right, God is going to answer the prayer which He has heard.

"Simon Peter, I have prayed for thee." That kept Peter from being another Judas Iscariot and committing suicide. He went out and wept bitterly, but he did not lay hands on his life, for the Lord prayed for him. Yes, and it was not very long until he was back to the Lord. How did Peter get back to the Lord? I will tell you how he got back. He went to the cross. Was Peter at Calvary? Yes! Because he says in his epistle he was an eyewitness (study it) of the sufferings of the Lord. I Peter 5:1. And as Peter stood under the cross, God restored his soul. There is nothing like a visit to Calvary.

THE CLIMAX OF PRAYER

Let us come to this last one in the twenty second chapter of Luke's gospel. "And when He was at the place, He said unto them, Pray that ye enter not into temptation. And He was withdrawn from them about a stone's cast, and kneeled down and prayed, saying, Father, if Thou be willing, remove this cup from me: nevertheless not my will, but Thine be done." There is the climax of His prayer. The climax of His prayer is the climax of all praying. "Not my will, but Thine be done."

When you kneel down before your God, when you are in the midst of some great circumstance, battle or conflict, when you can say "Not my will, but Thine be done, then you have learned the summit of intercession, and you have climbed the apex of the mountain of prayer with your glorious God. "A Look at Luke's Book." It is a Chronicle of Prayer!

TWO
LUKE'S GOSPEL - A COMPILATION OF PRAISE

I WANT TO BRING MY second message on "A Look at Luke's Book."

In our first message we found that Luke's book was uniquely a chronicle of prayer. I want to show you now that Luke's Book was uniquely a compilation of praise.

The book plumbs the very depths of sorrow. There is sadness here. There are deaths here. There are weepings here and tears here. There are also in this book dark moments of bitter frustration and disappointment. Yet in this book as in no other gospel, we climb the heights of ecstasy, joy and rejoicing. All through the gospel there are the depths of remorse, counterbalanced by the heights of rejoicing.

WOMEN IN LUKE'S GOSPEL

It would be absolutely impossible for me, in this message, to exhaust this subject. This is a subject which deserves the careful attention of everybody who studies the book. I am only suggesting the lines which need to be investigated and the themes which need to be exhausted. I must limit my study in this connection by considering the women of the book of Luke. Now Luke mentions certain women who are not mentioned in any of the other gospels. The gospels have their peculiarities you know. They have their uniqueness. There are things in one gospel which are not even mentioned in another. I will give you just one example. Nicodemus only occurs in the gospel according to John. You do not read about him in any other of the gospels. Now there are other characters who occur in one of the gospels and do not occur in any others. If you study carefully the gospel according to Luke, you will find that there are women mentioned in Luke's gospel who are not mentioned in any other gospel.

The women I particularly want to show you are women who had great sorrow. Something happened to them which overpowered them with sorrow. Yet in this gospel we see the sorrow dispelled, and the burden lifted, and the bitter disappointment taken completely away. From tears they are turned to joy, and from disappointment they are turned to praise.

ELISABETH, THE BARREN WOMAN

I am just going to give you the references to a few suggestions. In the first chapter we read about a woman, not mentioned in the other gospels, Elisabeth. In her we see a barren woman. Look at verse seven of chapter one, "Elisabeth was barren." Of course, as we know, among the people of Israel this was looked upon as a curse. A family that had no issue was looked upon as a family upon whom God had put His displeasure. You see, every Jewish woman wanted to be the mother of the promised Messiah. Thus, when a Jewish mother had no children, her grief was unbearable. You have an example of that in Hannah, have you not? You remember Hannah went into the tabernacle and she wept bitterly because she had no children.

Now if you look with me at verse twenty five you will find that Elisabeth herself said that this was a reproach. Now her husband, Zacharias, and herself were old and well stricken in years. Tugging at the heart's strings of Elisabeth was this bitter sense of deep disappointment. This gospel shows you how that burden was completely taken away. You know what she says here?

When she addressed Mary (look at it) she rejoices that God is able to do this thing, and she says: "Blessed art thou among women and blessed is the fruit of thy womb. And whence is this to me, that the mother of my Lord should come to me? For, lo, as the voice of thy salutation sounded in mine ears, the babe leaped in my womb for joy. And blessed is she that believed: for there shall be a performance of these things which were told her from the Lord." Here we have the barren woman becoming the mother of the greatest man ever born by human generation. For Jesus said there was not greater ever born of woman by human generation than John the Baptist. That is the first woman in Luke's gospel.

ANNA, THE BLESSED WOMAN

Now turn to chapter two and in chapter two you have another woman not mentioned in any of the other gospels. I am calling her the blessed woman. She also was a woman with a very great sorrow. Her name was Anna. She lived with her husband seven years, and at the end of the seven years she suffered deep bereavement. Her husband was taken from her. All the rest of her long life was lived in isolation and loneliness. Now in this chapter she is eighty-four years of age. Eighty-four years of age! What happens to her? God answers her prayers. We learned in our last message that Jesus came to this world as a direct answer to this old woman's prayer. What does she say? Look at it. Luke chapter two and verse thirty eight: "And she coming in that instant gave thanks likewise unto the Lord." She forgot about her own life of loneliness. She forgot about the bitter loss of her husband after seven years of marriage. Her lips overflow with the praise of the God of heaven.

Did I not tell you that this gospel is full of weeping, tears, deaths and sorrow? But did I not also tell you that counter-balancing those weepings and tears and deaths, are the praises of God.

THE WIDOW OF NAIN, THE BEREAVED WOMAN

Let us turn over a little farther. Let us come to chapter seven. Here is another woman not mentioned in any other of the gospels but uniquely mentioned in Luke's gospel. Verse twelve: "Now when He came nigh to the gate of the city, behold, there was a dead man carried out, the only son of his mother, and she was a widow." I hope you are getting the message. We have a barren woman in the first chapter. We have the blessed woman, who persevered in prayer, in the second chapter.

We come now to the seventh chapter and we have this woman whom I call the bereaved woman. She has lost her husband and all her heart's affections were wrapped around her only son. This woman was a woman who was well respected. Much people, we read, of the city was with her and the whole city was in mourning. She mourned and said: "I have lost my husband, but now I have lost my only boy." Do you realise how that woman felt as she was passing along with the mourners to the burying place? Now when the Lord saw her, He had compassion on her and said to her "Weep not, dry up your tears." This book of Luke is an epistle of death, weeping and sorrow, but it is also a gospel of rejoicing. What happened? "And He came and touched the bier: and they that bare him stood still." You remember when we were talking about the Lord's touch, that the touch of the Lord can stop funeral processions. When the Lord touched it, it stopped. What happened then? He said: "Young man, I say unto thee, Arise." (I would like to have seen the funeral undertaker's face that day. If he were a typical Jew he would say "I wonder will I get my pay for this funeral? I will have to put in at least half of my account anyway, for I tried to get this fellow buried.") "And he that was dead sat up, and began to speak." There is a beautiful little word here and I hope you have go it. "The Lord took him and delivered him to his mother." Was this not a nice introduction. The dead son raised, introduced again to his mother, by the Saviour. That is not it all however. I told you that this is a book which tells of rejoicing. "And there came a fear on all: and they glorified God." The weeping was gone and praise took its place.

THE SINNER OF THE CITY, A BAD WOMAN

You have a barren woman in chapter one and a blessed woman in chapter two. You have a bereaved woman in chapter seven. But look down chapter seven a little farther. There you have a bad woman, a woman of the streets (verse thirty seven) "And, behold, a woman in the city, which was a sinner." Yes! Here was a woman who had lost her virtue, a woman who had sunk down into the depths of the scarlet sin. Look what the old Pharisee who made the supper said. He said, (verse thirty nine) "This man, if he were a prophet, would have known who and what manner of woman this is that toucheth him: for she is a sinner." A bad woman! A base woman! but, thank God, Jesus Christ loves the greatest sinner. The old Pharisee had a hardened heart. He would not touch her with his fingertips. But there was room at the feet of Jesus for this sinner.

Thank God, we can say, "Jesus, what a friend for sinners, Jesus, lover of my soul. Friends may fail me, Foes assail me, He my Saviour makes me whole. Hallelujah! What a Saviour. Hallelujah! What a Friend, saving, helping, keeping, loving, He'll be with me to the end."

What did the Master say to this woman? He said, verse forty eight, "Thy sins are forgiven." She came in that day a bad woman, and she went out like Anna, a blessed woman. Her sins were all forgiven. This is related only in Luke's gospel and is not to be confounded with the anointing of Jesus' feet by Mary the sister of Martha. So do not mix up the two incidents.

JOANNA AND SUSANNA, BEDEVILLED WOMEN

Let us come to chapter eight, and you have two other women here, not mentioned in any other of the gospels: "Joanna the wife of Chuza, Herod's steward. And Susanna, and many others, which ministered unto Him of their substance." Now we read of them as, "certain women, which had been healed of evil spirits." These were bedevilled women. Mary Magdalene is mentioned along with them, but she is also mentioned in the other gospels. These two, Joanna and Susanna, are not. Both of them had the devils in their hearts. In verse two of chapter eight it says, "They had infirmities." Poor bedevilled women, with the devil within them and with infirmities of their bodies, as the result. Then Jesus came, and when Jesus came, something happened! How do I know it happened? Because it says it in the previous verse. Have a look at it. Verse one "The glad tidings of the kingdom of God." Weeping, depression, disappointment, oppression of the devil are all lifted when Jesus comes. At the glad tidings the devil fears and flees.

MARTHA, A BUSY WOMAN

Look at chapter ten and verse thirty eight. Here is a lovely little narrative about Mary and Martha. You do not find it in any other of the gospels. "Now it came to pass, as they went, that He entered into a certain village: and a certain woman named Martha received Him into her house. And she had a sister called Mary, which also sat at Jesus' feet, and heard His Word. But Martha was cumbered about much serving." This is a busy woman. A busy woman! She was busy about much serving. Is it wrong to be busy? NO! But it is wrong to be cumbered. You see if your business has mastered you, you are finished but if you have mastered your business you are on the top. Yes, and I admit freely, some days my work does get on top of me. Yes! Then everything goes against me. Of course, you would not know anything about that! But I know about it. There might be a few people here honest enough to say "That is right, I have experienced that." You get up in the morning and everything goes against you. You are in a hurry to shave and you cut yourself. Yes and when you come downstairs you do not like the breakfast which your wife has made for you, and you are as crabbed and as crooked as you can be. Is that not right? And women, do not laugh, for you can just be as crabbed too!

Aye, we are cumbered. It ought not to be, but it happens, does it not? That is why I like the gospels, they are so true to fact. Here is a busy woman, cumbered, overcome. Her work is on top of her. Now the Lord is very gentle with her. You know what He says? He says: "Martha, Martha, thou art careful and troubled about many things." It has got on top of her. "But Mary has chosen that good part."

If you are so busy you have not time to sit at Jesus' feet and hear His Word, you are too busy. It is time you took stock and sat down. "One thing is needful, and Mary has chosen that good part."

THE WOMAN OF THE SYNAGOGUE, THE BOWED DOWN WOMAN

The last woman I want to show you is in chapter thirteen and verse ten: "And He was teaching in one of the synagogues on the Sabbath. And, behold, there was a woman which had a spirit of infirmity eighteen years, and was bowed together, and could in no wise lift up herself. And when Jesus saw her, He called her to Him, and said unto her, Woman, thou art loosed from thine infirmity. And He laid His hands on her: and immediately she was made straight, and glorified God. And the ruler of the synagogue answered with indignation, because that Jesus had healed on the Sabbath Day," (what crooked perverts they were), "and said unto the people. There are six days in which men ought to work: in them therefore come and be healed, and not on the Sabbath Day. The Lord then answered him and said, Thou hypocrite, doeth not each one of you on the Sabbath loose his ox or ass from the stall, and lead him away to watering? And ought not this woman, being a daughter of Abraham, whom Satan hath bound, lo, these eighteen years, be loosed from this bond on the Sabbath Day? And when He had said these things, all His adversaries were ashamed: And all the people rejoiced for all the glorious things that were done by Him."

I could preach a good gospel sermon on that. The way I would preach it would be very simple. This woman came of the right stock, but she was just as twisted in her nature as any other sinner. She was a daughter of Abraham. She had the blood of the right genealogy in her veins, but Satan had got the hold of her.

YOUR LINEAGE DOES NOT COUNT, YOU ARE STILL A SINNER

I want you to notice that nobody else in the church could do anything for her. She came to the synagogue, and even that old hypocrite, the minister we would call him, got all worked up when she was healed. He could not do anything for her. There is nobody in the church who can make a sinner straight. There is only one person can do that, and that is Jesus.

And I want you to notice something. She did not call for Him. He called for her. That is what we call, in the Reformed Calvinistic Faith, the effectual call of the gospel. When I preach the gospel, there is a general call. In that general call sometimes there is an effectual call. As a result some man sitting in the pew says "He drew me and I followed on, Charmed to confess the voice divine." Do you remember the day you heard that call?

Old John Bunyan in his House of the Interpreter showed a hen with her chicks. She made a general call and nothing happened. When she made a peculiar call however every chicken came and hid under her wings. Old Bunyan quaintly says "There is a general call that no one heeds, not even the chick. But when old mother hen gives that special call, they come running for safety under her wings." Happy is the man, who has heard that call!

"Jesus called her to Him." That is not enough. You must come into contact with Jesus. "He laid His hands on her and immediately she was made straight." It was not like some of these healing people that tell you you are healed, and you're no better than you were. This was immediate healing! Complete and absolute healing! Now when the Lord heals you, He heals you immediately. Do not mistake me. I believe the Lord can heal today. I have seen Him healing people and doing the job completely. But when God does it, there is nothing counterfeit about it. It can stand up to the test. It can indeed.

Do you know what happened? She glorified God! She stood up in the church for the first time after eighteen years, straight as a ramrod, and she gave her testimony. So you know what happened? What always happens - sinners go mad. The old clergyman went mad. I remember leading a man to the Lord once, and he went back to see his minister, and the minister danced with anger on the doorstep of the manse when he told him he was saved. But when he said he was saved through Paisley, that made the dance far worse.

This is a great story of conversion. Is it not? The bowed down woman made straight. Have I not showed you that Luke's gospel is a compilation of praise? Go and read it for yourself. There are others in it, I have not exhausted it. We just got to chapter thirteen. Seven women. We started with weeping, and we ended with joy. We started with burdens and we ended with the burdens lifted.

And if you have come into this service and you are a sinner and you have a burden or you are a Christian and you have a burden, let me tell you, God can wipe away the tears today, and give you joy unspeakable and full of glory.

THREE
LUKE'S GOSPEL - A COMPENDIUM OF POWER

THE FIRST THING WHICH we noticed about Luke's book is that it is a chronicle of prayer. You will find more references in Luke's book than in any other of the gospels, to the Lord Jesus Christ at prayer.

In our second study we discovered that Luke's book was a compilation of praise. We noticed in the book of Luke that there are certain women who are not mentioned in the other gospels. Women with a great burden who had great sorrow, and great afflictions. Yet when the Lord came He turned their darkness into light, their midnight to midday and their mourning into songs of praise.

So we find that, uniquely, Luke's book is both a chronicle of prayer and a compilation of praise.

A COMPENDIUM OF POWER

Now we want to consider Luke's book as a compendium of power. If you have your Bible, and you turn to Psalm sixty two and verse eleven you will read these very important and striking words: "God hath spoken once; twice have I heard this; that power belongeth unto God." Power belongeth unto God!

In any study of the scriptures there is a very important law which should be kept in mind. It is called the law of progress. When a doctrine is announced in scripture, or an important prophetic theme, the whole of the prophecy or the whole of the doctrine is not revealed at once. The Bible teaches line upon line, precept upon precept, here a little and there a little. So there is a progress in the divine revelation. First the blade, and then the ear and then the full corn in the ear. That is the way which the Scriptures teach their sublimest truths.

If you look into the gospels you will find this illustrated. For instance, the Lord Jesus Christ, in Matthew's gospel, reveals to His disciples that He is going to die. Look at Matthew sixteen and verse twenty one. There the Lord Jesus Christ is revealing His death. Of course, this came as a great shock to the disciples. They thought He was going to sit down on His Father David's throne, and they were going to be royal courtiers around the throne.

Matthew sixteen and verse twenty one: "From that time forth began Jesus to shew unto His disciples, how that He must go unto Jerusalem, and suffer many things of the elders and chief priests and scribes and be killed, and be raised again the third day." This was the first announcement to the disciples that He was going to die.

THE LAW OF PROGRESSIVE REVELATION

Turn over to chapter seventeen and verse twenty two. He there reveals something further to them "And while they abode in Galilee, Jesus said unto them, The Son of man shall be betrayed into the hands of men" "Betrayed" is not mentioned in the previous chapter. Now He tells them about the betrayal. He then goes on to tell about His killing. He does not say what way He is going to be killed. He only says He is going to be killed. Then He goes farther, and He tells them now about His resurrection.

Turn to the twentieth chapter. Notice first of all He tells them He is going to be killed. Then, He adds in chapter seventeen that He is going to be betrayed. When we come to chapter twenty and verses eighteen and nineteen, He says: "Behold, we go up to Jerusalem." Chapter twenty and verse eighteen: "and the Son of man shall be betrayed unto the chief priests and unto the scribes, and they shall condemn Him to death." Then there is a further revelation: "And shall deliver Him to the Gentiles" (it did not say this before in the previous prophecies) "to mock, and to scourge, and to crucify Him: and the third day He shall rise again." So now He reveals the death and the awful happenings which surrounded that death.

If you turn to the twenty sixth chapter, He tells them there something more. Verse thirty one, "All ye shall be offended because of me this night." He prophesies the complete forsaking of His Person by all His apostles.

So you will notice the progress which is made in the gospels. Everything is not revealed at once. Now not only are the contents of the gospels progressive but the books of the gospels themselves are progressive. We are making progress from Matthew to John.

HUMAN RELATIONSHIPS IN THE FIRST THREE GOSPELS

In Matthew's gospel Christ is presented as the embodiment and fulfiller of the Old Testament scriptures. When you are studying Matthew's gospel, you will find over and over again it says, "This was done that it might be fulfilled which was spoken by the prophet." So Matthew begins the story of Christ's life by showing that Christ fulfilled the Old Testament prophecies. He is seen in Matthew as the son of Abraham.

When we come to Mark's gospel there is no genealogy. Mark is the gospel of the Servant. No one worries about the servant's parentage. All that is important about the servant is the job which he does. So there is no genealogy in Mark's gospel. Mark reveals Him as the Servant. When you are studying Mark's gospel note the "immediately's". He did everything immediately. He was not a slothful servant. He was a faithful servant.

In Matthew He tests the people of Israel concerning His claims. In Mark He ministers to the people of Israel as the servant of Jehovah. So we are progressing.

In Luke's gospel we have a different picture of Christ altogether. In Luke's gospel He is the Son of man. His ministry goes beyond the borders of Israel to the whole world. You have the Gentile emphasis in his gospel. He is seen as the perfect Man, the Son of man. He is the son of David and Abraham in Matthew. He is the Servant of God in Mark. He is the Son of man, the Saviour of the world in Luke.

The first three gospels are all dealing with human relationships, His relationship to us. In Matthew He is King! In Mark He is the Servant. In Luke He is the Saviour. He is our King, He is our Servant, and He is our Saviour.

JOHN'S GOSPEL DIFFERENT

But when you come to John's gospel emphasis is no longer upon a human relationship. It is a divine relationship. In John's gospel He is the Son of God, the Son of the Father.

Now keeping this in mind, if you look at the end of every gospel you will find that there is progress. The law of progress is manifested. Matthew's gospel ends with His resurrection. Mark's gospel speaks about His ascension. Luke's gospel ends with the promise of Pentecost. John's gospel, however, ends with the promise of His coming again. There is the progress from resurrection to ascension, to Pentecost and to His coming again. So the four gospels dovetail completely into one another because man did not write them. It was God Who inspired them.

We turn now to Luke's gospel as the compendium of power. Luke presents the Lord Jesus as the Perfect Man. There was one other perfect man upon the earth one day. His name was Adam. He was made perfect. He was put into the Garden of Eden, and he was put under the test. He was put into the place of trial and he fell. In his fall he carried down the whole human race. He lost for us the right of access, the right of approach, the right of fellowship with God. You remember what happened. God drove out the man, and placed at the entrance into Eden's garden a cherubim with flaming sword, keeping the way to the tree of life. By Adam's fall heaven was closed, approach and access were blocked up. Man stood in the place of banishment and in a place of rebellion from the Throne of God. But I want to show you something. In Luke's gospel, uniquely, heaven is opened. Once again business is done between heaven and earth.

HEAVEN IS OPENED IN LUKE'S GOSPEL

Look at the first chapter of Luke's gospel, and you will find that heaven is opened in the very first chapter. There is a visitant from heaven to earth. Zacharias is doing his work as a Levite. What happened? "There appeared unto him an angel of the Lord." You will notice what the angel told him. He said in verse nineteen: "I am Gabriel, that stands in the presence of God." The presence of God was banned to man by Adam. In the coming of the last Adam all this is reversed. This is very important, you know. The Lord Jesus Christ is not the second

Adam, He is the last Adam. The Lord Jesus Christ finished everything that had to do with Adam in regard to the curse. He finished it all. Adam brought a curse. The last Adam saved us from that curse and redeemed us from that curse. Christ is called, in scripture, the last Adam, but He is also called the Second Man. He is not called the last man, He is called the Second Man.

Why? Because He is the beginner of a whole race of second men, men who have been born a second time. I hope you get it. He is the last Adam, for He has finished, Hallelujah, the curse which fell in Eden. He is the beginner of a new race of second born men, men who have had a second birth.

Now Gabriel said that he himself stands in the presence of God. Heaven is opened. Communication is now re-established. Look further down this chapter, and you will find Gabriel comes back a second time. Verse twenty six: "And in the sixth month the angel Gabriel was sent from God (notice the wording very carefully) unto a city of Galilee, named Nazareth." Heaven is opened again, Hallelujah! There is a Man, a perfect Man on His way, and before He comes, God announces, communication is re-established. It was re-established to announce the forerunner, re-established to announce His Own incarnation and His Own first advent.

HEAVEN COME DOWN TO EARTH

Let us turn over a little farther. We will find in chapter two and verse nine, that "the angel of the Lord came upon them: and they were sore afraid. And the angel said unto them, Fear not: for behold, I bring you good tidings of great joy." Look at verse thirteen: "And suddenly there was with the angel a multitude of the heavenly host." A multitude of the heavenly host! Here we find the entire inhabitants of heaven come down to earth among men. Why? Because Jesus Christ, the perfect Man has been born. I am emphasising His humanity now. He is not only perfectly and impeccably man, but thank God He is perfectly and impeccably God. In Luke's gospel however, we are bringing out His blessed humanity.

HEAVEN OPEN AT OUR LORD'S BAPTISM

Heaven is opened. That very expression "an open heaven" is used when we come to the beginning of Christ's public ministry. What did the Lord Jesus Christ come to do? He came to save men from their sins! He came to re-establish an approach road to God. Thank God, there is a way back to God from the dark paths of sin. There is a door which stands open, that all may come in. At Calvary's Cross, that is where you begin, when you come as a sinner to Jesus. Jesus Christ began His public ministry at His baptism. Chapter three and verse twenty one of Luke's gospel: "Now when all the people were baptised, it came to pass, that Jesus also being baptised, and praying (read it) the heaven was opened." I want you to notice something, that the first visitants along this approach road were angels. They were the first visitants. We see the ministry of angels in chapter one and in chapter two. An angel came to Zacharias An angel came to Mary. Angels came to the shepherds in the field.

Now Jesus is entering His public ministry. Notice He enters the same way He made His exit. Baptism is a perfect type of death, burial and resurrection. When the Lord Jesus Christ was about to enter His public ministry, He went through the symbolic act of dying. He was put under the Jordan waves and He came up dripping with the water of Jordan upon Him, "and heaven was opened." There is a difference. It was not angels who came then.

It was the Holy Ghost Who came. Look at it: "And the Holy Ghost descended in a bodily shape like a dove upon Him." Power belongeth unto God.

The power which you can have is the power of access, the power to approach to God. If you have got that power, then you have got God's friendship and you have got God's ear. Everything you ask of God is answered. That is the greatest power which any man can have. Happy is the man who has the ear of the Almighty. Happy is the man who can approach the Almighty. "Who shall ascend into the hill of God, He that hath clean hands and a pure heart." The greatest blessing you can have, the greatest power you can have is to be able to approach to God.

When Jesus Christ came out of the Jordan wave, the Spirit of God came down and abode upon Him. God spoke. There was an open heaven with an open voice.

FIRST TIME SINCE ADAM'S FALL

It was the first time after the fall that God could look down upon a man and say he was well pleased with Him. You know when God created man He was pleased with him. "God saw that it was good." From the day of the fall however, God could never say it was good. Here once again on earth is a perfect Man. He has lived all His life in absolute perfection. Thirty years of age He now is. He has fulfilled every letter of the law. Remember this was not at the beginning of His life but this was at the beginning of His public ministry.

Thirty years had gone, and the eye of God had been on Him from His birth, through His childhood, in the carpenter's shop and through all His sojourn in Nazareth. For thirty years He was in isolation. From twelve to thirty there is not one word about Him. God's eye was upon Him and at the end God said: "This is my beloved Son; in whom I am well pleased." Heaven is opened, the Holy Spirit has come. I want to tell you something.

We, who are in Christ, have the same experience. For if you are saved, heaven has been opened to you. Thank God, the Spirit of God has descended along the approach road and abides within your heart. He came and He abides for evermore the same, The Father, Son and Holy Ghost, all Blessed be His Name. Not as a transient guest, not at set times or tides. The Holy Ghost He came to me, He came and He abides. God looks at you today in His Son and says: "Thou art My Son." "For as many as received Him, to them gave He power to become the sons of God, even to them that believe on His Name."

SAINTS COME DOWN FROM HEAVEN

In Luke chapter nine and verse twenty eight, you will find an open heaven again. This time there are two more visitors from heaven. It is getting better you know. First of all, angels come, then the Holy Spirit comes, and then the saints of God come. Two of them! Who were they? Moses and Elias. I want you to notice that they appeared in glory with Him. It is worth studying carefully every syllable and every word. "They appeared in glory." Moses and Elias represented all the Old Testament saints, Moses - the law. Elias - the prophets. There they are. They have now come down by the approach road. Heaven is opened.

And what did they talk about? They talked about the thing which made it all possible. They talked about His decease, His death, which He should accomplish at Jerusalem. They met that day around the cross on the top of the mount. "Jesus, keep me near the Cross, there a precious Fountain, free to all, a healing stream flows from Calvary's mountain. In the Cross, in the Cross, be my glory ever, till my raptured soul shall find rest beyond the river." Do you know what that was a type of on the mountain? That was a type of the day when we will all be glorified.

There was danger however. Peter fell into wrong thinking and wrong doctrine. He elevated Moses and Elias to the same plane as Christ, for he said, "Let us make three tabernacles, one for Thee, one for Moses and one for Elias." Then the cloud came, and when they lifted up their eyes it was "Jesus only." There are not three tabernacles. There is only one tabernacle, and that tabernacle is Christ alone. "The Word became flesh, and tabernacled amongst us, and we beheld His glory." No other glory! The Lamb is all the glory in Emmanuel's land.

THE FINAL OPENING OF HEAVEN

I want to tell you something. If you go to the last book of the Bible, you will find the day when heaven is opened finally. Let us look at it, just in finishing. By the way, I have not exhausted my theme. You can go through the whole of Luke's gospel, and you will find that heaven is opened. At the very end of the book, heaven is opened forever. For the Lord said: "Tarry at Jerusalem, until you are endued with power from on high." Here is an open heaven for the church! The power of Pentecost comes down that great approach road to earth.

The twenty first chapter in the book of the Revelation: "And I saw a new heaven and a new earth: for the first heaven and the first earth were passed away; and there was no more sea. And I John saw the holy city, new Jerusalem, coming down from God out of heaven, prepared as a bride adorned for her husband. And I heard a great voice out of heaven saying, Behold, the tabernacle of God is with men."

Do you know that every important thing in the Bible has a signpost hanging outside it. It is the word "behold". Whenever you read that word "behold" in the Bible, something of great importance is coming.

THE WORD "BEHOLD"

The doctrine of total depravity. How is it stated in the Bible? "Behold, I was born in sin, and shapen in iniquity." The virgin birth: "Behold, a virgin shall conceive, and bear a Son." The day of salvation: "Behold, now is the day of salvation." The Lamb of God: "Behold, the Lamb of God." Here is another one: "Behold, the tabernacle of God is with men, and He will dwell with them." "He will dwell." We are back to Eden, Hallelujah! We are back to a greater than Eden. It is a new heaven and a new earth. All that was lost in Adam and more is gained in

Jesus Christ. For after all, at best, Adam was only a gardener. But we, praise God, are going to dwell in the temple of God and become kings and priests. "Behold, the tabernacle of God is with men, and He will dwell with them, and they shall be His people, and God Himself shall be with them, (great company) and be their God. And shall wipe away all tears from their eyes."

An open heaven and a perfect Man. Thank God, there is a Man in the glory, the Man of Calvary. He has won my heart from me, He died to set me free. Blest Man of Calvary!

FOUR
LUKE'S GOSPEL - A COMPANION OF PILGRIMAGE

IN OUR FIRST MESSAGE, we saw that Luke's book was a Chronicle of Prayer. It is the gospel which tells us more about the prayer life of the Lord Jesus Christ, than any other gospel.

In the second message, we saw that Luke's gospel is a Compilation of Praise. We saw seven women, not mentioned in any of the other gospels, women who had great sorrow, women whose sorrow was turned into joy, and whose weeping was turned into praise, by the touch of the Master's hand.

MOSES AND ELIAS - WHY?

In our third message, we saw that Luke's gospel was a Compendium of Power. It is the gospel of the open heaven. Angels came down out of an open heaven. The Holy Ghost came down out of an open heaven at Christ's baptism.

Moses and Elias came down out of an open heaven. Why Moses and Elias? Why not Joshua and Jeremiah? Why not two others of the Old Testament prophets and leaders? I will tell you why. Because Moses died and was buried. God buried Moses. He is a type of all those saints of God that fall asleep in Jesus, which God will bring with Him.

Elias did not die. He went up to heaven, "in a chariot of fire." No he did nothing of the kind. The chariot of fire did not take Elijah up to heaven, he went up to heaven by a whirlwind. The chariot of fire is a type of the abiding presence of God. That never leaves the saints of God. Elisha said "Open the young man's eyes." And when he looked he saw the chariots of the Lord round about Elisha. The chariots remain with us. The Lord's presence! He went up in a whirlwind. He is the type of the saints who will not die. When Jesus comes, there will be people who will not die. They will be caught up to meet the Lord in the air, after the dead in Christ rise first.

There are a lot of Christians and they say "I hope that will happen to me, and I never will need to die." I want to tell you if it does happen to you it will be a wonderful experience. You will, however, be robbed of one thing. You will be robbed of the victory over death. You will never be able to say, when you get to heaven, "I knew what it was to die and pass through the valley of the shadow, and have the Lord's presence there."

I think if I had a choice to make, I would rather die and have that experience, and then I could boast about it to you throughout all eternity!

Moses and Elias are types of the church redeemed. That is why it is Moses and Elias. The open heavens! The book is a Compendium of Power!

THE COMPANION OF PILGRIMAGE

The last thing I want to look at is that Luke's gospel is the Companion of Pilgrimage. Luke's gospel is a book of pilgrimage. God's people in Luke's gospel are always travelling. They never become part and parcel of the order of things. They are never part of the establishment. They are always outside the camp. They are always travelling forward, and travelling onward, travelling Godward and, Hallelujah, travelling homeward. It is a book of travel!

The Lord Jesus Christ is seen in this book as the great Pilgrim and God's people are seen on a pilgrimage.

THE FACT OF THE PILGRIMAGE

The first point I want to make is the Fact of the Pilgrimage. Secondly, the Feast of the Pilgrimage, because there is a particular feast in this book which is described in an unusual manner. The last supper is described uniquely in Luke's gospel. Thirdly, the Fire of the Pilgrimage. Fourthly, I want to talk about the Finale or the Finish of the Pilgrimage.

Now let us look at the first one; the Fact of the Pilgrimage. Turn over to Luke's gospel chapter three. This is the beginning of the ministry of the Lord's forerunner. In verse one and two you have the establishment. You have all the governors and tetrarchs in their places. That is the political establishment, is it not? All in its place. Then in verse two you have the religious establishment in its place too. Annas and Caiaphas are the high priests. So you have the state and you have the church and the establishment all in their places. There is noting disturbed, everything in the garden seems to be rosy.

JOHN THE BAPTIST A DISTURBER

Then if you look with me at the end of verse two, you will find that the Word of God came unto John. Where was he? Where was God's man? Was he in the establishment? No, sir! Was he part of the political setup? No sir! Was he part of the religious setup? No sir! He was in the wilderness. He was outside the camp. That is where he was! He was not in the establishment. He was a pilgrim.

If you go down the chapter to verse nine, do you know what he says? He says "And now also the axe is laid unto the root of the tree." If you study the work of a prophet, you will find that the work of the prophet has two ingredients. One, to expose the present order of things and, secondly, to expect a new order of things. They both go together. When a man is a prophet he exposes. John the Baptist is only a pilgrim. He is in the wilderness. He is not part of the establishment. The establishment eventually cut off his head.

THE MINISTRY OF THE MASTER

Now come to the ministry of the Lord Jesus after His baptism. Luke chapter four. The first place into which the Spirit led Jesus was the wilderness.

If you read this book of Luke, go through it and mark all the times when the wilderness is mentioned. This is the wilderness book. This is a book of pilgrimage. Let me tell you something. As I have been studying the book of Luke, I have discovered another thing. I have discovered that the whole life of Christ is a series of anticipations of His death, burial and resurrection. In Christ's life there are great milestones or crises. Campbell Morgan once wrote a very valuable book, and if you can get a copy of it do get it.

It is called "The Crises of Christ." A very good book indeed! There are crises in the life of Christ. Every great crisis however in the life of Christ is a preview, is an anticipation of His death, burial and resurrection. They are, as it were, photograph previews of the end of His pilgrimage.

Let me illustrate it for you. At the start of His personal life after His birth - what happened? There was death! Do you hear the marching soldiers of Herod intent to slay Him? What happened to Him? He was carried down into Egypt. Egypt is a type of the world but Egypt is also a type of death. The first time in the Bible a coffin is mentioned it is mentioned in regard to Egypt.

Turn with me to the last verse of the last chapter of Genesis: "So Joseph died, being an hundred and ten years old: and they embalmed him, and he was put in a coffin in Egypt." Egypt is a type of death.

THE END OF GENESIS AND THE END OF EXODUS

May I just suggest to you that there is a great difference between the last verse of Genesis and the last verse of Exodus. Genesis is the book which tells of our ruin, and it ends in a coffin. That is where sin brings us. Sin when it is finished bringeth forth death. Turn now to the last verse of the book of Exodus. Exodus is the book of redemption. If you look at the last verse you will not read about a coffin there. What will you read about? You will read about a cloud there. A cloud! Yes! "For the cloud of the Lord." "The cloud of the Lord." Ruin by sin ends in the coffin. Redemption by blood ends in the cloud. We shall be caught up in the clouds to meet the Lord in the air, so shall we ever be with the Lord.

The second coming of Christ is always associated with the clouds. "He shall come in the clouds, with great glory." Go and study it for yourself. The book of redemption therefore ends in the clouds. Thank God, we are going higher some day. Where then did they take the Lord Jesus Christ to? To Arabia? No! They took Him down into Egypt, a type of burial, and when old Herod was dead, Christ was brought up out of Egypt, a type of resurrection. "Out of Egypt I have called my Son."

PREVIEWS OF OUR LORD'S DEATH

So at the beginning of His personal life, you had in symbol death, burial and resurrection. What was the beginning of His public life? The beginning of His public life was His baptism. In His baptism you have a perfect type of His death. Jordan is a type of death. He was baptised in Jordan, which is a type of burial.

When He came up, heaven was opened. God spoke. The Holy Ghost descended, a perfect type of resurrection. So at the beginning of His personal life, death, burial and resurrection, in type. At the beginning of His public life; death, burial and resurrection, in type.

What was the next great crisis in His life? The next great crisis in His life was the transfiguration. If you study Luke's gospel and the transfiguration, you will find that there is a type of death there also. The apostles went to sleep. Sleep in the scriptures is a type of death. On two occasions, Peter, James and John went to sleep. They went to sleep on the mount of transfiguration. They went to sleep in the garden of Gethsemane. A type of death.

Two men appeared unto them on the mount of transfiguration. What did they talk about? They talked about the decease that He should accomplish at Jerusalem. The conversation on the mountain was His death. Ah, but you say: "Preacher, how do you get the type of burial on the mount of transfiguration?" If you put on your spectacles and read the Bible carefully, you would see it quite clearly. You know, Peter got excited on the mountain, and he said: "Let us make three tabernacles, one for Thee, one for Moses and one for Elias." That was a sinful thing which Peter said even although he was in the mount of blessing. Elias and Moses are not equal with the Lord Jesus Christ. What happened? A cloud came. A cloud! Three men went into the cloud, the Lord, Moses and Elias. When the cloud passed over, however, they saw no man save Jesus only. Why? Because Jesus alone is the real conqueror of death. He is the only One who comes forth victorious from the burial. Yes and immediately that happened, heaven was opened. That is resurrection.

So the whole life of Christ is a series in type of death, burial and resurrection. In fact, the whole gospel is one of pilgrimage.

THE FEAST OF PILGRIMAGE

But let us turn to chapter twenty two and there you will find the Feast of Pilgrimage. It is a wonderful chapter. I would love to be able to spend time upon this man who led the way, carrying the pitcher of water. Some might say "Well that was a strange thing that the Lord said." He said in verse ten: "Behold, when ye are entered into the city, there shall a man meet you, bearing a pitcher of water." Surely there could be hundreds of men bearing pitchers of water. How would we know the right man? The answer is simple, because there would not be hundreds of men bearing pitchers of water, it was the women who carried the water. Do you remember the woman of Samaria went to carry the water? That was the habit of the Jews. They made the women do the work. The women carried the water. Do you not see that this was a unique man!

What did the Lord say? Verse eleven: "Where is the guestchamber?" That is very important. What is a guestchamber? It is the place where the guests stay for a night, and then go on. It is not a permanent residence. It is only the guestchamber. This is the feast of the pilgrimage.

THE TWO FEASTS OF PILGRIMAGE

There were two feasts in the guestchamber that night. There was the passover. The passover was a feast of pilgrimage too. At the passover, the shoes were on the feet, the loins were girded about, and the staff was in the hand. Immediately the passover was finished, the children of Israel left Egypt. They were pilgrims! The feast which Jesus left for His church also is a feast of pilgrimage. It is limited in its duration. It is only "till He come". We need to capture, as we sit around the table, the atmosphere of the guestchamber. We are only staying here for the night. Praise God, the morning is about to dawn, and the saints are going home to the Father's house for all eternity. It is a feast of pilgrimage, in the guestchamber, just for a night, just for a little season. Then, praise God, the Master will come, and call for us.

THE FIRE OF PILGRIMAGE

Let us pass on to the last chapter of Luke's gospel. Two men on a pilgrimage, going to Emmaus. They are just like us, are they not? When we are going on a pilgrimage it could be said of us what was said of them in verse seventeen: "What manner of communication are these that ye have one to another, as ye walk, and are sad?" That is like God's people at times. As they walk down the road of life, if you looked at their faces you would know that they were sad. Why? Because life is full of sorrow, life is full of sadness, life is full of disappointments, life is full of heartaches and heartbreaks. They are sad.

This book however is the Companion of Pilgrimage. There comes a stranger along. A stranger! He joins Himself with them. He walks with them, and He rebukes them. How often we need the rebuke of God. He says: "O fools, and slow of heart to believe." That is what is wrong with us all, we are slow of heart to believe. The curse of unbelief is within our hearts. "To believe all that the prophets have spoken." "All."

Then He sat down with them. I wonder why He was made known to them in the breaking of bread. You know, the Eastern man had a garment that was loose and it covered his flesh altogether, you could not see his hands. As they sat down at the table, He took the break and brake it and they saw His hands. They were nail-pierced hands. Immediately their eyes were opened, and they knew Him. Notice how the conjunction carries it over "Blessed it, AND brake, AND gave to them, AND their eyes were opened." Yes! They knew Him! Did you know what they said? Here is the Fire of the Pilgrimage. "Did not our heart burn within us?" "Burn within us."

As you and I walk down the road of life, we need the comfort of God, do we not? Our hearts are sad. I had a very sad happening this week in my own home. Last weekend, my father just sat in his old chair and wept. He wrote on a little piece of paper to me that he wanted to go and see his mother's grave. So on Wednesday my brother-in-law, James Beggs and myself took him down to Sixmilecross in County Tyrone. He led me in through the churchyard gate and up the little braeside of the old burying ground. He took me to the place where his father and mother were buried, and there he stood and wept. Then we had a word of prayer together, and we left, and his sorrow was imparted to me. We were sad.

But I said to him on the way home, "There is a day coming, father, when all will be well, the family circle, in grace, will be united in Christ." And he dried up his tears, and patted me on the shoulder, for he cannot speak, and he nodded his head in approval. The Lord had drawn near and our hearts burned within us. Let the Lord come near you, and He will cheer your heart today, burdened soul. Is there some burdened one in the meeting? Praise God, your heart can be cheered for there is the Fire of Pilgrimage.

THE FINALE OF PILGRIMAGE

In this last chapter there is the Finale of Pilgrimage. Verse fifty three: "And were continually in the temple, praising and blessing God. Amen." That is what is going to happen in heaven. You shall be a pillar in the house of our God, you will neither go out nor in, but you will be there forever. "Continually in the temple, praising and blessing God." That is the finale of it all. When we all get to heaven. What a day of rejoicing that will be, when we all see Jesus, we will sing and shout the victory.

Amen and Amen

3 The Blood
of the Lamb

A SERIES OF FIVE SERMONS ON THE BLOOD OF THE LAMB, PREACHED IN THE MARTYRS MEMORIAL CHURCH, BELFAST AT THE ANNUAL EASTER CONVENTION IN 1976. THE SUBJECTS ARE: THE VOICE OF THE BLOOD, THE VIRTUE OF THE BLOOD, THE VITALITY OF THE BLOOD, THE VALUE OF THE BLOOD AND THE VICTORY OF THE BLOOD.

ONE
THE VOICE OF THE BLOOD

IF YOU HAVE YOUR Bible, would you turn to the twelfth chapter of Hebrews.

There is an important law in all Biblical interpretation. My people are well versed in this law, because I do not know how often, in my preaching, I have emphasised and underlined it. It is the law of the first mention. That is, the first time a doctrine, a person, a word, or a particular truth is mentioned in the Bible it gives you the golden key to every other mention of that particular doctrine, person or truth. So in keeping with that law I open my Bible to find the first mention of the blood.

You will find it in Genesis chapter four and verse ten. Carefully notice that the first person in the Bible to mention the blood is God Himself. That is very significant. The first Person to mention the blood in the Bible - God Himself. He said, "What hast thou done? the voice of thy brother's blood crieth unto me from the ground."

Learn, firstly, that the blood has a voice.

Learn, secondly, the blood has a loud voice. It cries as it speaks.

Learn, thirdly, the blood has a voice which God hears. He says, "Thy brother's blood crieth unto me." God heard it.

Fourthly, learn that the blood cries from the place of the curse. "It crieth unto me from the ground."

The third chapter of the book of Genesis and verse seventeen reads, "Cursed is the ground for thy sake. Thorns also and thistles shall it bring forth to thee." Where did the blood cry from? It cried from the place of the curse. It cried from the place of thorns.

That is very significant. Of course, everything about the Bible is significant, instructive, intriguing and interesting.

Now the gospel lesson from Genesis chapter four and verse ten is found in Hebrews chapter twelve and verse twenty-four, "And to Jesus the mediator of the new covenant, and to the Blood of sprinkling, that speaketh better things than that of Abel."

I want to open this series with a short message on "The Voice of the Blood."

We want to look, on the Lord's Day morning, at "the Virtue of the Blood." On the Lord's Day evening we are going to look at "The Vitality of the Blood." On Monday morning we are going to look at "The Value of the Blood," and in the evening at "The Victory of the Blood of Christ." So we have a tremendous theme.

We are looking now at the voice of the Blood, "the Blood of sprinkling speaketh better things than that of Abel."

We have three points. First of all I am going to *Number the Context.* Secondly, I am going to *Name the Comparison and the Contrast,* and, thirdly, I am going to *Note the Content.*

FIRST, NUMBER THE CONTEXT

First of all we will number the context. Look with me please at verse twenty-two (Hebrews 12: 22) and you will find that this is one of the mountain texts of God's Word. It has to do with Mount Sion. If you look carefully at verses twenty-two, twenty-three and twenty-four you will discover there are seven things about Mount Sion. I will tell you the way you will find them (they are difficult to find in our Authorised Version). The way to find them is to note the "ands". Look at verse twenty-two, "ye are come unto Mount Sion, *and,* (that marks the first one) unto the city of the living God, the heavenly Jerusalem, *and* to an innumerable company of angels, to the general assembly *and* church of the firstborn, which are written in heaven, *and* to God the Judge of all, *and* to the spirit of just men made perfect. *And* to Jesus the mediator of the new covenant, *and* to the Blood of sprinkling that speaketh better things than that of Abel."

I looked up my Greek Testament this afternoon and I discovered something I never knew before, that the general assembly has not to do with the church of the firstborn, but has to do with an innumerable company of angels. You will notice there is a comma after angels and in the original the word "to" is not there. It reads, "to an innumerable company of angels, the universal or general assembly."

SEVEN GREAT FACTS

You will notice something about those seven things, that they are a double seven. I tell you, when God does it He does it well. There is a double seven.

You will notice that "the city of the living God" is further described as "the heavenly Jerusalem."

I would like to have time to preach on these sevens. Turn them over in your mind and you will discover that the first man that looked for a city was an old man called Abraham. He looked for a city. What city did he look for? "A city which hath foundations, whose builder and maker is God." What city is that? It is the city of the living God, the heavenly Jerusalem.

Then you will notice "the innumerable company of angels" - "the general assembly." A double description. The innumerable company of angels, the general or universal assembly. Then "the church of the firstborn" (then the double part of it) "which are written in heaven." or, reading very literally, "whose names are recorded above."

That is good, is it not? I am glad my name is written there on that page bright and fair. Hallelujah! Praise the Lord! My name is written there!

Let us look at it, "to God" (then He is described as the Judge of all), "the Judge of all," and to "the spirits of just men - made perfect." (Notice the double description.) And to "Jesus" - "the mediator of the new covenant," and to "the Blood of sprinkling" - "that speaketh better things than that of Abel." You are going up the mountain!

NOTE THE ORDER

I want to show you something. In the sevens in the Bible, one and seven go together. Two and six go together. Three and five go together. The centre one is the fourth one, three to one side and three to the other. Who is the centre here? The centre is God the Judge of all.

If you look at the last one you will find that the last one is the Blood, and the first one is the city. The city of the living God, the heavenly Jerusalem, is founded on the Blood of the Lamb. That is what it is built on, the Blood of the Lamb.

Then you have the innumerable company of angels, linked with Jesus the mediator of the new covenant. Then you have the church of the firstborn, linked with the spirits of just men made perfect. God, the Judge of all, in the centre.

I want you to notice that the Blood is the seventh. It is the summit of the mountain. It is the culmination. You start with the city. You go on from the city to the angels, and from the angels to God. Then from God to the spirits of just men made perfect, to Jesus and the final topmost summit of the mountain is the Blood of sprinkling.

Now start off at the entrance to the Tabernacle and you have an Altar there, you have a Laver there, and you have the Holy Place there, with the Table of Shewbread, the candlesticks and the golden incense altar before the Veil. Part the veil, and at the parting of the veil you have the ark of the covenant and the mercy seat. What caps the mercy seat? The last thing the high priests did, he sprinkled it with the blood of the lamb, the blood of the atoning sacrifice.

Thank God, as we number the context of our text we find the Blood is the summit.

What do they sing about in Heaven? What is the top note that they strike in the song of eternity? "Unto Him who loved us and washed us from our sins in His own Blood. To Him be the glory."

SECOND, NAME THE COMPARISON AND THE CONTRAST

THE COMPARISON

Now I want to name the comparison and the contrast. The blood of Abel and the Blood of Christ. Let us compare them. *Firstly,* Abel was a shepherd and the Lord Jesus Christ was a shepherd. It is the cry of the shepherd's blood.

Jesus Christ is depicted in scripture in three ways. He is the Good Shepherd. That illustrates His office as Priest. "He giveth his life for the sheep." He is the Great Shepherd. "That Great Shepherd of the sheep." That illustrates His office as a Prophet. "Working in us that which is well pleasing in His sight." And He is the Chief Shepherd. That illustrates his office as King. "For when the Chief

Shepherd shall appear He shall receive a crown of glory that fadeth not away." He is the Good, Great and Chief Shepherd.

Secondly, Abel died a death of violence at the hands of a blood relation.

Christ died a death of violence at the hands of His own nation. "He came unto His own and His own received Him not."

Thirdly, the blood of Abel cried and God heard it. The Blood of Christ cries and God hears it.

Fourthly, the blood first cried from the place of the curse, from the ground that brought forth thorns. The blood of Abel fell on thorny ground.

The Blood of Christ stained the thorns which He wore. If you look up at the Cross tonight and stand under its shadow, the topmost thing on that Cross is a crown of long eastern thorns which pierce His brow, and every one of them is stained crimson with the Saviour's Blood.

That is the comparison. Let us look at the contrast.

THE CONTRAST

Abel died by force. Christ died as a willing Sacrifice. Abel died as a sacrificer, offering the lamb on the altar. Jesus died as the Sacrifice. The voice of Abel's blood cried for revenge. The voice of Christ's Blood cries for remission. The blood of Abel polluted the ground. The Blood of Christ is preserved in Heaven for evermore. The blood of Abel was lost. The Blood of Christ lives on and shall never lose its power. It is upon the very Throne of God itself. (You can check that in Hebrews chapter nine verses eleven to fourteen.) "But Christ being come an High Priest of good things to come, by a greater and more perfect tabernacle, not made with hands, that is to say, not of this building. Neither by the blood of goats and calves but by His own Blood."

The high priest took a basin of blood of goats and calves and he went into the Holiest of All and sprinkled the mercy seat. But Christ (Hebrews chapter nine and verse twelve) "by His own Blood."

What did Jesus Christ take with Him? His own Blood! The Body of Christ did not see corruption. Neither did the Blood of Christ see corruption. As the Body of Christ was resurrected and went to Heaven, so the Blood of Christ was resurrected and Christ took it with Him to the glory. What did He do with it? You read there what He did with it. "He entered in once into the holy place, having obtained eternal redemption for us." Verse thirteen, "For if the blood of bulls and of goats, and the ashes of an heifer sprinkling the unclean (mark the words "sprinkling the unclean") sanctifieth to the purifying of the flesh, how much more shall the Blood of Christ (that is the second Person of the Trinity) Who through the eternal Spirit (there is the third Person of the Trinity) offered Himself without spot to God (there is the first Person of the Trinity, the Trinity united in the Blood-shedding and offering and purging of the Blood of Christ) purge your conscience from dead works to serve the living God?"

In the mystery of redemption, if the earthly things were sanctified and cleansed by earthly sacrifice, the heavenly places themselves by greater sacrifices than these. By the Precious, Precious Blood. Listen, we are not redeemed with corruptible things. The Blood never corrupted. The Blood of Jesus never congealed. If you lost your blood tonight it would congeal and become solid, but the Blood of Jesus never congeals, it still flows as fresh as ever from the Saviour's wounded side. Hallelujah!

> *None need perish,*
> *None need perish,*
> *All may live for Christ has died.*

THIRD, NOTE THE CONTENT

Last of all, let us note the content of what it says. It says "it is the Blood of sprinkling." Those are wonderful words "the Blood of sprinkling."

There are three great instances in which the Blood was sprinkled. Go back to the Passover night. The Israelites were told to take the basin of the shed blood. They were told to take hyssop and sprinkle the blood upon the lintel and the sideposts of the door, the entrance to the house. There is a word used there that is used nowhere else about the blood. It does not say "sprinkled," although it was sprinkled. It says, "Strike the doorpost!" "Strike the lintel!"

Thank God that is what the Blood of Jesus did for me. It struck the lintels of the posts of Heaven. It struck the doorposts of glory. When it struck them, the door opened for me, and praise God, I walked in sheltered under the Blood of the Lamb. I believe there is *Striking Power* in the Precious Blood of Christ. What a day when the Blood struck your heart, brother. What a day that was, when God saved us by His Son's Blood.

THE TWO-FOLD WORK

On that day when he consecrated the priests, Moses sprinkled them with the blood. Look at chapter nine and chapter ten of Hebrews and you will find that. You will find here in chapter nine and verse nineteen a cross reference in the Old Testament, Exodus chapter twenty-four verses six to eight. There you will discover that the blood was divided in half. (Very interesting.) He was to take half the blood and apply it Godward. He was to take the other half and apply it manward.

Thank God the Blood of Christ has a two-fold work. It works Godward and It works manward. And as It works Godward It speaks. What does It speak? It speaks to God. God bends over His ear and He says "What do I hear? It is the voice of the Precious Blood of my Precious Son." Yes, and if God heeded the voice of Abel's blood crying for vengeance, how much more does He heed the voice of the Blood of His Blessed and Holy Son? Praise God He listens to that voice.

But half of that Blood works manward, "Peace, perfect peace in this dark world of sin, The Blood of Jesus whispers peace within." It speaks peace to my heart.

I noticed something today which I never noticed before. Verse nineteen of Hebrews chapter nine, Moses took the blood of calves and of goats, and he mixed it with water. If you read the First Epistle of John you will find, He came not only by blood but by water. When they put the riven spear into the side of Jesus there flowed forth Blood and water. Yes!

They took hyssop (the hyssop was a root out of a dry ground, the little wilderness plant), a type of the humanity of Christ. They took the scarlet wool (you get it from the lamb's back, from the sheep's back). "He was led as a lamb to the slaughter, and as a sheep before her shearers is dumb." The lamb's wool, however, is white, but they were to take scarlet wool, that was, the wool which was dyed. The scarlet colour is the royal colour. Christ was a Royal Lamb. The Lamb who died for me was God's Royal Lamb. I tell you who He was, He was God. He wore the scarlet robe of Deity. Praise God, He became the hyssop and the scarlet wool for me. What happened? It was sprinkled both on the book and on all the people.

THE BLOOD SPRINKLED BOOK

Do you know how you were saved? You were saved through a sprinkled Book. Do you see that Book, it is stained with the Blood of Jesus right through. You could not pinprick the Body of that Divinity but the Blood would run out of it. It is full of the Blood. Every chapter of every book speaks about the Blood. Blood in Genesis, Blood in Exodus, Blood in Leviticus, Blood in Numbers, Blood in Deuteronomy, Blood in Matthew, Mark, Luke and John. Blood in Malachi. Blood in the Revelation. Blood in the prophets and Blood in the epistles. It is the Book of Blood.

Out of the window of this Book, and out of the window of the harlot Rahab there hangs the crimson tassel of the Saviour's Blood. You know what happens? When you read the sprinkled Blood, your heart becomes sprinkled with the Blood of Jesus. Oh, you get the touch of the Blood of the Lamb upon your heart and upon your soul.

The other reference is on the great day of atonement. Before the High Priest was permitted to sprinkle the Blood on the Mercy Seat, he had to put up the incense. The incense had to cover the Mercy Seat. You know what the incense speaks of? It speaks of the Holy Life of Jesus. He offered Himself as a sweet smelling incense to God.

I could not approach the Mercy Seat in which there is the law of God, but I can approach it when the Holy Life of Jesus covers it. Yes, and when the Holy Life of Jesus covers it, then I can know the power of the sprinkled Blood of the Lamb in my heart and in my life.

THE BETTER THINGS

Let me show you, in closing, something else. A great little thought. It says here concerning this Blood, "It speaketh better things!" If you read the book of Hebrews you will find there are a whole lot of "better things." Just turn to Hebrews chapter eleven and verse sixteen and you will find these words, "But now they desire a better country."

A BETTER COUNTRY

Do you see Abel? I see him. He is standing at the gate of Eden. The cherubim's sword touches the lamb which he is offering, and the fire consumes the sacrifice. Many times Abel stands there and looks into the Paradise which is lost. He longs to get into that Paradise again. But God says, "I have a better Paradise for you. I have a better place for you than that. I am going to transfer that tree of life from

Eden into Heaven." Yes, and there is a day coming, you read about it in the Revelation, when there is a better country, that great City where the tree of life grows in the midst of the Paradise of God. "Abel, I have a better country for you. Not Eden, it is the Eden above. Not an earthly garden, but rather the City of God." The Blood speaketh better things. It speaks of a better country.

I am glad I am not going to be here forever. Some day I will finish the course. Some day, please God, I will fight the last battle and I will have run my race. God will then say, "Come up higher," and the Lord will say "Welcome home."

What a better country we are going to. They will never mutilate the hillsides of Glory with the gravedigger's spake. No hospitals yonder. No shrouds or coffins there. No pain or aches. No death dew or death rattles. Praise God it is a better country. The Blood speaketh better things. It tells me tonight of a better country.

A BETTER RESURRECTION

If you turn over to Hebrews chapter eleven again you will find there is another better thing in this chapter. Verse thirty-five, "that they might obtain a better resurrection." A better resurrection! There are three "betters" in this chapter. Three is the number of completion. So in this eleventh chapter, the great faith chapter, there are three "betters." Here is the second one, "a better resurrection."

Abel knew that he was going to die some day. God said to his father, "Dust thou art and unto dust thou shalt return." Abel was the first man to die.

I remember my father saying, "As Adam and Eve saw the dead body of Abel, for the first time they realised what God meant by death. They had not seen a man die before. But as they stood over the body of their son they learned what death was."

Abel was the first man to die, but God had a better resurrection for him.

I think that Abel must have felt very strange when he got over into the Glory Land, because he was the only disembodied spirit there. There were angels there but there were no other human beings there. He was the first saint to make it. When he got there, God told him that there was going to be a better resurrection. God said, "Abel, that body that Cain slew, it lies corrupting in the ground, but one day it will rise again." A better resurrection! "The blood of sprinkling that speaketh better things than that of Abel." A better country! A better resurrection!

A BETTER THING

Look at verse forty, "God having provided some better thing for us." That is the best one of all, is it not? Those old warriors from Abel right down to the last one, they were great old warriors. God has something better for me. I have been privileged to live in the dispensation of Grace. The prophets longed to see this day. They did not see it. John the Baptist longed to see this day, and he did not see it. "He that hath the bride is the bridegroom."

Praise God, we live in a day when all the scales have fallen away, and we see the power of the Precious Blood of the Lamb. Those Old Testament saints never saw it fully. "God having provided some better thing for us."

A better country, a better resurrection and a better thing for us. The Blood of sprinkling!

I trust that you will once again, when you go home, number the context, name the comparison and the contrast, and note the content. Remember, there is power in the Blood of Christ.

May God bless this little Bible study. May God help us to hear the vocal Blood of Christ speaking tonight. Up yonder in heaven it is speaking. In my heart it is speaking. "Precious, Precious Blood of Jesus, Oh, receive it; Oh, believe it; 'Tis for thee."

TWO
THE VIRTUE OF THE BLOOD

IN THE PREVIOUS STUDY we called on the help of the great principal of Biblical interpretation, the law of the first mention. And if you turn to Genesis chapter four and verse ten you will find the first mention of the Blood in the Bible is God himself. And He said, "What hast thou done? The voice of thy brother's blood crieth unto me from the ground." And we learned a great truth, that the Blood of Christ is vocal, because we compared that scripture in Genesis chapter four and verse ten to Hebrews chapter twelve and verse-twenty four. There we read that the Blood of Jesus speaketh better things that that of Abel.

You will notice four things about that Blood and its first mention.

Firstly, the Blood has a voice, it lives after death, Hebrews chapter eleven, the first three verses. It says there, "he being dead yet speaketh" in reference to Abel.

Secondly, the Blood has a loud voice. It cries.

Thirdly, the Blood crieth from the place of the curse, from the ground, "Cursed is the ground for thy sakes, thorns shall it bring forth." And of course, the Cross was the place of the curse. There were thorns upon His brow at Calvary. But, thank God, the Blood cries from the place of the curse.

We want to come from the Blood vocal, or the voice of the Blood, this morning to the Virtue of the Precious Blood of Christ.

When I speak of the Virtue of the Blood, what do I mean? I refer to the Blood of Christ in its essential character, its basic nature. I speak of its intrinsic goodness, its innate purity and its moral potency, and its incorruptible liquidity, the Precious Blood of Christ.

Now, of course, the Blood owes its Virtue to the Person from whose veins it flowed. The Blood can never be divorced from its Donor. And if your turn to Revelation chapter seven you will find there a great expression, the expression of the redeemed around the Throne of God in Glory. And what do they shout? They shout, "Washed in the Blood of the Lamb, washed in the Blood of the Lamb."

Now, there is another great rule in biblical interpretation which I want to call into help us this morning. It is the rule and law of development. What does that mean? It means this, that the Bible does not reveal the whole truth about this subject right away. It reveals it little by little, line upon line, precept upon precept, here a little, there a little. And so there is a progress in the revelation of Divine Truth. Jesus said "First the blade, then the ear, then the full corn in the ear." So there is the law of development or the law of growth in the Bible.

As I study the Lamb in the Bible, I find there is a sevenfold unveiling of the Lamb in the Bible. Starting from Genesis and going right through to the book of the Revelation there is a seven-stage unveiling of the Lamb, and we are going to look at the Lamb in relation to the Virtue of the Lamb's Blood. Because, as I have already said and let me underscore it and underline it again, the Blood owes its Virtue to the Person from whose veins it flows. And the Blood can never be divorced from its Donor.

Turn to the Book of Genesis, and to chapter twenty-two. It is the story of Abraham and Isaac. They are going on a journey, and as they go on this journey Isaac has a question to ask. He says in verse seven, "Behold the fire and the wood, but where is the lamb?" "Where is the Lamb?" Here is the first stage in the revelation of the Lamb in the law of development in the Bible. "Where is the Lamb for a burnt offering? And Abraham said, "My son, God will provide Himself a Lamb for a burnt offering."

Could I just give you a little aside here. You can study it out for yourself. If you look at verse five of Genesis chapter twenty-two you will find the first reference in the Bible to worship. You will find that Abraham said to the young man, "Abide ye here with the ass; and I and the lad will go yonder and worship, and come again to you." And you will find three things essential to true spiritual worship.

Firstly, look at verse four, "Then on the third day." It was on the third day. The third day is the day of resurrection. He rose again the third day, according to the scriptures. And all spiritual worship is on the basis of the Lord's resurrection.

The whole system of Romanism is a system founded on a dead Christ. A Christ hanging on a crucifix. A Christ helpless in the tomb. A Christ weak and impotent in His mother's arms.

The whole basis of true Biblical Christianity is, Christ is alive. Jesus is a living Saviour. May we worship Him in the basis of the resurrection.

Secondly, you will notice that they had to separate. The true basis of worship is separation. "Stay thou here, I am going yonder to worship."

I want to say, if we are going to worship God we have got to say to our companions, we have got to say to our business, we have got to say to our relations, "Stay thou here, I am going yonder to worship." some of us in this church have known the bitter cost of having to say that. We have had to stand outside the camp of ecclesiastical establishment in order to go to worship.

Thirdly, you will notice this about it, that Abraham was going to give his all. He was taking Isaac and he did not think that Isaac would be with him when he returned, and yet there was faith in his heart. He believed that God could give a resurrection. So he was taking with him his all to leave on the altar.

If I am going to worship God this morning I have to leave my all on the altar.

That is only on the side, that has nothing to do with the message! But I wanted to give you those thoughts for I am sure they will be a blessing to you, and you can work them out more fully.

ONE: THE PROVISION OF THE LAMB

Let us come to verse eight, "God will provide Himself a Lamb." You can write over that "the provision of the Lamb."

Man stands impotent in the face of sin. Man is ruined. He cannot rebuild the ruin. Man is in rebellion. He cannot bring to an end that rebellion. A way must be found whereby man in ruins can be regenerated, and man in rebellion can be reconciled to God, Hallelujah, for God has provided the Lamb. And in that God-provided Lamb you have an emphasis placed on the virtue of its Blood, because it was the virtue of the Blood of the Lamb that was Divinely provided.

Turn over to Exodus. Notice the development! The twelfth chapter of Exodus. It is a wonderful portion. It is well worth your study. Look at verse three of the twelfth chapter of Exodus and you will see, "they shall take to them every man a lamb" notice the indefinite article, "a lamb". Then come to verse four, "And if the household be too little for the lamb." Notice the definite article there, "the lamb." In verse three it is "a lamb". In verse four it is "the lamb". Then look in verse five, it is "your lamb."

There was a time when I was in the world, and God's Lamb was only "a Lamb" as far as I was concerned. Then there came a day when God opened my eyes and I saw He was "the Lamb," the only One. And then, thank God, there came a day when I could say He is "my Lamb."

Thank God for those in this congregation who can say "He is our Lamb." Praise God He is ours!

TWO: THE PURITY OF THE LAMB

Look at it. Verse five, "Your lamb shall be without blemish, a male of the first year: ye shall take it out from the sheep, or from the goats." Read down the chapter and you will find it has to be taken out for a double period of perfection, for two sevens. It was to be separated fourteen days. That is the first thing. The second thing, it is without blemish.

Christ is Holy, Harmless, Undefiled, Separate from sinners. Now there is a great testimony to the Purity of Christ in the New Testament. The apostle Paul has something to say about that. He says in II Corinthians chapter five and verse twenty-one, "For He hath made Him to be sin for us (note it) Who knew no sin." The Purity of the Lamb, "Who knew no sin."

Peter says, in his epistle I Peter 2: 22, "Who did no sin."

Paul says, "He knew no sin." Peter says, "He did no sin." John says (I John 3: 5) "In Him was no sin."

I want you to note that testimony, "He knew no sin." "He did no sin." "In Him is no sin." When that Blood of Christ was released, that Blood was absolutely Pure. It is the Sinless Blood of Christ. It takes its Purity from the Purity of the Lamb. Notice, He Hath made of one blood all the nations of the earth. No difference between the blood of any race. it is all the same. But Christ's Blood is not the blood of a poisoned, fallen race. Thank God the Blood of Christ is Pure, and Spotless, and Crimeless, and Harmless and Sinless. The Sinless Blood! Thank God for the Purity of the Lamb.

THREE: THE PERSON OF THE LAMB

Turn over now to Isaiah. (You will notice how it is building up.) You had the Provision of the Lamb. "Where is the Lamb?" Then you have the Purity of the Lamb. Now we come to the Person of the Lamb. Isaiah chapter fifty-three and verse seven, "He is brought as as lamb to the slaughter."

The Jewish people were so filled in their worship with symbols and types and shadows that they might have come under the impression that this Lamb was another ordinary sacrificial lamb.

God is revealing the truth, line upon line, precept upon precept, here a little and there a little.

Now He says, the Lamb is a Person. "He is led as a lamb to the slaughter." If you look at Isaiah chapter fifty-three you will find there the Person of the Lamb, and what a Person He is.

Look at verse two, "For He shall grow up before Him as a tender plant, and as a root out of a dry ground."

It is impossible for any root to grow out of any ground that is absolutely dry. This refers to the Virgin Birth of Christ: He is a root out of a dry ground. But He is also a tender plant. He is God Himself. "He hath no form nor comeliness: and when we shall see Him, there is no beauty that we should desire Him." That is the Person of the Lamb! "He is despised and rejected of men, a man of sorrows and acquainted with grief: and we hid as it were our faces from Him; He was despised, and we esteemed Him not."

What a Person! He is Divine. Washed in the Blood of the Lamb! The Lamb Provided. The Lamb that is Pure. The Lamb that is the Person. And what Person? The Person of the Son of God.

FOUR: THE PURPOSE OF THE LAMB

We come to the New Testament, and in John chapter one and verse twenty-nine we have the great cry of John the Baptist. "Behold, the Lamb of God, which taketh away the sin of the world."

You can write over that scripture. "the Purpose of the Lamb." What was His purpose? Why did He come? He came to put away sin. Jesus purposed to put away sin. The means He used. He in His omniscience knew He would be adequate to do the job. The Blood of Christ has no insufficiencies and it has no inefficiency. The Blood of Christ can do the job that God intended and purposed that it would do. There is the purpose of the Lamb.

I want you to notice the progress that we are making: The Lamb is Provided. The Lamb is Pure. The Lamb is a Person. The Lamb has a Purpose.

FIVE: THE PRECIOUSNESS OF THE LAMB

Let us come a little further. And we come now to I Peter chapter one and verse nineteen, and there we find another great statement about the Lamb - a very important statement about the Lamb. "Forasmuch as ye know that ye were not redeemed with corruptible things, as silver and gold, from your vain conversation received by tradition from your fathers. But with the precious Blood of Christ, as of a Lamb without blemish and without spot." (I Peter 1: 18)

There you have the Preciousness of the Lamb. And now Precious is that Lamb. It is the Preciousness of the Lamb that gives the Preciousness to the Blood.

What makes a thing precious? *First of all, a thing is precious because of its uniqueness and scarcity.* If a thing is very scarce and very unique, it becomes precious.

How unique is God's Lamb! He is the only One. There is no one else like Him. No friend like Him is so High and Holy. No, not one. No friend like Him can meet our needs. No, not one. He is Precious because He is the only One.

Secondly, a thing is precious when it becomes the object of your affections. When your love is set upon it.

I have got some children. They are precious to me. They might not be precious to anybody else. Other people might want to give them a good scud on the ear; but they are precious to me. (I give them an odd scud myself.) But they are precious to me, because my love is set upon them. That is why!

How Precious is Jesus! Do you know who set His love upon Christ? God the Father. And do you know that on two occasions while Christ was on earth, God could not restrain Himself, so He shouted down from heaven until men heard, "This is My Beloved Son." He was Beloved of the Father.

I will tell you something else. He is Precious to me today because I love Him. I love Him because He first loved me. I love Him because He first loved me!

Then, of course, preciousness results from age. The older the thing is, the more precious it becomes. The longer its history, the more precious its nature.

Who is the Lord Jesus? Thank God, He is the Ancient of Days. Before time began He was in the Father's bosom. He never had a beginning. He is the unbeginning Beginner. And He made all things, and He was before all things, and by Him all things consist. He is Precious because of His age.

Then, lastly, preciousness results from association. We have little things at home that are not precious to anyone else. But, because they belonged to our father and our mother, they have stored in them precious memories. And when we look upon them we stir those memories, our hearts are strangely moved and strangely blessed.

What precious memories we have of Jesus!

> *"Lest I forget Gethsemane,*
> *Lest I forget Thine agony,*
> *Lest I forget Thy love for me,*
> *Lead me to Calvary!"*

And that Precious Lamb has shed Precious Blood. That is the virtue of the Blood, its Preciousness! Bought with the Precious Blood of Jesus.

SIX: THE POTENCY OF THE LAMB

Turn to Revelation chapter five and verse six. I want you to notice the progress we are making. We are going to the summit. We are going up the hill. At the foot of the hill we ask the question, "Where is the Lamb?" God provides it. It is a Pure Lamb. It is the Person of Christ, and Christ alone. Then we discover it has a Purpose, and that purpose is to take away our sins. Then we find it is Precious, the Precious Blood of Jesus, Revelation chapter five and verse six. "And I beheld and lo, in the midst of the throne and of the four beasts, and in the midst of the elders, stood a Lamb as it had been slain." You read the context, "John wept because no one could open the Book, and look thereon." "And one of the elders saith to me,

Weep not: behold, the Lion of the Tribe of Juda, the Root of David, hath prevailed to open the Book, and to look thereon." You can write over it, "The Potency of the Lamb."

"O, the Lamb, the Bleeding Lamb,
O, the Bleeding Lamb,
He was found worthy."

And, there is power in the life's Blood of that Lamb! You will notice that the vision of the throne is of a Lamb that was slain, a Lamb in association with His Blood.

SEVEN: THE PRIMACY OF THE LAMB

Then we come to the last one. In that last one we reach the climax. the last mention of the Lamb in the Bible. There is a double reference, Revelation chapter twenty-two, "And He shewed me a pure river of water of life, clear as crystal, proceeding out of the throne of God and of the Lamb. In the midst of the street of it and on either side of the river, was there the tree of life, which bare twelve manner of fruits, and yielded her fruit every month: and the leaves of the tree were for the healing of nations. And there shall be no more curse: but the throne of God and of the Lamb shall be in it." A double-fold reference to the throne of the Lamb. You can write over that "The Primacy of the Lamb." He is first. The highest place that heaven affords is His by sovereign right! He takes the primacy in heaven. What virtue is in this Blood, the Blood of the Lamb! Who is a co-occupier with the God of Heaven in the Holy Throne of the Holy Trinity of the God of all wisdom, of all grace and of all power! The Primacy of the Lamb.

We have seen the seven-fold development of the revelation of the Lamb. When I stand at yonder Cross and when I gaze upon the Precious Blood of Christ, I can say "When the Atonement story first began, a Lamb was Sacrificed for every man. And then when Israel was in Pharaoh's land, the Lamb could for a household stand. Later a Lamb at the atonement feast was offered for the nation by a priest. But last on Calvary's Hill the Lamb of God shed for a sinning world His Precious Blood. A Lamb before the world's foundation slain, and in the farthest future just the same. For in the Revelation we are shown the Lamb has been slain, amidst the throne. A Lamb, the pivot of earth's history, God's great impenetrative mystery. Thou hast redeemed us by Thy Precious Blood. And made us kings and priests unto our God. Worthy the Lamb that once was slain, will be our praise throughout Eternity. Singing, Washed in the Blood of the Lamb."

THREE
THE VITALITY OF THE BLOOD

I WANT TO SPEAK on a great subject, "The Dynamic behind the empty tomb, or the Vitality, the living Efficacy, the life-giving merit of the Blood of Christ."

You will find my text in Hebrews chapter thirteen and verse twenty. It is one of the great prayers of the apostle Paul, "Now the God of peace, that brought again from the dead our Lord Jesus Christ, through the Blood of the everlasting covenant."

We learn there that Jesus Christ was brought again from the dead and that Jesus Christ is the great Shepherd of the sheep. The raising of the Shepherd and the return of Jesus from the dead was accomplished by the power, by the instrumentality, by the motivation of the Blood of the everlasting covenant. The whole emphasis of the Bible on the great doctrine of our redemption is redemption by the Blood of Christ.

Turn to Genesis and you will find there Paradise lost. And when Paradise was lost, how did God clothe our fallen, naked, shamefaced, first parents? He shed the blood and He made coats of skin and clothed them.

Turn to the Book of the Revelation. Look at the great company around about the Throne. Who are these? Whence came they? These are they that have washed their robes and made them white in the Blood of the Lamb.

The garments of Paradise lost are the garments of Blood. The garments of Paradise regained are the garments of Blood. And from Genesis to Revelation, every book in the Holy Volume, every chapter in every book, every verse in every chapter in every book is dyed crimson with the Blood that is drawn from Emmanuel's veins. This is a crimson, Blood-stained volume. And God, with indelible writing, has written in crimson capitals, in one short, final, ultimate sentence, the great truth of the law of redemption, Hebrews nine and verse twenty-two, "Without the shedding of Blood there is no remission."

When I turn to the doctrine of the Saviour's Blood I discover there is a three-fold principle which underlines that great doctrinal truth.

Turn over to the Book of Leviticus, a very important book and there is a very important verse in that book. Leviticus chapter seventeen and verse eleven. In this text you have a three-fold principle which underlines the whole teaching of the Blood that saves, the Blood that redeems, the Blood that brings remission, the Blood that pardons, the Blood that cleanses, the Blood that covers, the Blood that justifies, the Blood that sanctifies and the Blood that glorifies. "For the life of the flesh is in the Blood."

THE VITAL PRINCIPLE: THE BLOOD IS THE LIFE

There is the first cord in the three-fold principle ("the life of the flesh is in the Blood"). What is it? *The vital principle, the Blood is the life.*

You know, to many of us the idea of blood speaks of death. But I want to tell you that nowhere in the Bible, and this is a strong statement, does the Blood of Christ refer only to His Death. It refers not only to His Death but to His Life. And the idea of Blood is not the idea of death, it is the idea of life.

Of course I learn that from the symbolism of the Old Testament economy. You will remember the priest could not enter the Holy Place to do service if he had come in contact with death. You know that. Once he touched something that was dead he was immediately polluted. He had to be cleansed before he could approach the Holiest of All. What happened on the great day of atonement? On the great day of atonement the priest took the blood in the basin. Does that blood not speak of death? No! In the mind of God it speaks of life beyond death? It speaks of a life that defies death. It speaks of a life that triumphed over death. It speaks of a life that strangled death and put death to death, and triumphed in all its mighty potency and in all its tremendous power. And he carried living blood into the Holiest of All.

Thank God some of us know that the Blood is the life, for there was a time when we were dead in sin. There are men in this church tonight and they lay in the grave. I remember, sir, when you were in the grave of your sin. I remember when you were a hopeless drunkard. I remember when some of you were caught up with the gambling fever. I remember some of you when you were down and out in your sin. And when I came to this road thirty years ago you were running with the Devil's crowd to Hell. What happened? The Blood touched you. What did it do? It brought you to life. Hallelujah! Man, there is power in the Blood of the Lamb. There is a wonder-working power, death destroying power in the Precious Blood of the Lamb. God help us to preach it, and to magnify the Blood of Christ.

There was an old professor in Princeton seminary, when Princeton seminary, the great school of Presbyterianism in the United States, was a bulwark for truth and orthodoxy. When the students graduated, the old professor used to get up at this desk and face the students and say, "Young man, make much of the Blood of Christ in your ministry (one of the times I was in America I went to Princeton to see the desk that he stood at). Make much of the Blood of Christ in your ministry. Preach up the Blood." Hallelujah! May God help us to preach up the Blood tonight!

The Blood is the life, the vital principle.

THE VICARIOUS PRINCIPLE: THE BLOOD IS THE LIFE GIVEN

Look again at verse eleven, "And I have given it to you upon the altar to make an atonement for your souls." There you have the vicarious principle. The Blood is the life given veraciously. What do I mean by that? Substitutionary - instead of me.

Here I am. I deserve the Infinite wrath of God. I deserve Hell's destruction on my soul and body for all eternity. I deserve to crawl into the nethermost pit of Hell and feel the fire of brimstone upon my body and soul that is stained, and soiled, and ruined, and diseased and filled with the cancer of sin. That is all I deserve. But, thank God, there was One Who came, and, thank God, on the Cross He gave His life for me. The Blood is the life.

The Blood is the life given. Who did He give it for? He gave it for every soul that will put his trust in Him. If you put your trust, sir, in Christ tonight, I do not care how dark your sin is, how vile your life is: I do not care how deep you have gone into the hovels and kennels of dirty, filthy sin, He will wash you and make you whiter than the snow. He will make you so clean that you will be fit for the company of Heaven and the company of God for all eternity.

This is God's salvation we are talking about tonight. You could not get this at a baptismal font. You could not get this at a Communion Table. You could not get this by joining a church or being a Protestant. Thank God you can get this if you are washed in the Blood of the Lamb. Come on, friend. Have you been to Jesus for the cleansing power? Are you washed in the Blood of the Lamb? Are you fully trusting in His grace this hour? Are you washed in the Blood of the Lamb?

THE VIVIFYING PRINCIPLE: THE BLOOD IS LIFE-GIVING

Look at the last principle, "For it is the Blood that maketh an atonement for the soul." There you have the vivifying principle. What is that? The Blood is the life. That is the vital principle. The Blood is the life given. That is the vicarious principle. The Blood is life-giving. That is the vivifying principle. It makes an atonement for the soul.

A man that comes unatoned cannot worship God. He stands outside the tabernacle. He has no way of access. He is out of communion, he is out of touch, he is not linked with God. Then the blood of the sin offering, it is offered. The blood is sprinkled on the horns of the altar. The priest makes an atonement for his soul. And that man who was reckoned to be dead is now reckoned to be alive. That man who was reckoned a rebel, is now reckoned to be reconciled. That man who was going to Hell is now reckoned to be going to Heaven. What has happened? The vivifying principle has operated in his heart. The Blood is life-giving. It gives life.

Having said that, let me come to the Cross of the Lord Jesus Christ.

SUBSTITUTION AND RESTITUTION

There are two things about the Cross of Christ. When Jesus Christ died there was *substitution*. He took my place and died for me. But when Jesus Christ died there was *restitution*. He did something. I have broken the law. I have offended God. Reparations had to be made to the Almighty. The debt had to be paid. God's Truth had to be honoured. God's Purity had to be vindicated. God's Justice had to be exonerated. Thank God, with His Blood there was made restitution for me. All that I had done to offend God finds its answer through the Blood of Christ. All that guilty shame, all the terrible debts, all the hideous past, all the hellish thoughts, all the heinous nature, praise God it is fully, totally, absolutely answered. Where? In the Blood of Christ! He has made a full restitution for my soul.

There are two things that you must remember about the Blood. It is not only *a life given for men,* but, thank God, it is *a life given to men.* The Blood is not only the Blood that is shed, but, thank God, it is the Blood that is sprinkled.

THE FIRST THREE REFERENCES TO BLOOD

Now, let me show you something. This basic idea of Blood. You say, "You have not come to your subject yet." I am getting to it. I am going a long way. I am not coming directly to the Ravenhill Road, I am going round by Ballymacarrett; I will get there all right! The first three references to the Blood in the Bible emphasise this great idea of the vitality of the Blood, that there is life in the Blood.

Let us glance at Genesis chapter four and verse ten. Abel is dead. He cannot speak any more; no, but something is happening. The Blood is speaking. What does that mean? It means there is life after death through the Blood.

That is what Jesus did for me at the Cross. He, on the Cross, brought to me life after death. "He being dead yet speaketh." If He speaketh, then He is not dead. Thank God, tonight *there is life after death in the Blood.*

Then if you turn to Genesis chapter nine and verse four you will find again that the Blood is life. That is set out in the principle of the covenant with Noah.

Turn to Exodus chapter twelve and verse thirteen you will find that the Blood preserves the life. "When I see the Blood I will pass over you." You will not die!

I have often wondered at the Jewish father. He goes out with his little boy (I think of it many times. I think of how I would feel if I took my firstborn out by the hand), for a walk to the flock and there takes out a little lamb, a little woolly creature. "We are going to keep the lamb for fourteen days." And the little boy would say, "Why, daddy?" Because that little lamb is going to die for you. If you do not have that lamb killed, you will be killed. And when the fourteenth day came the father took his firstborn, and he slaughtered that little lamb and he preserved all its blood for the blood was infinitely precious. He put it in a basin. And then he took a piece of hyssop and he put the hyssop into the blood and struck the sideposts of the door and the lintel of the door. He made a crimson archway. And he said, "Now, son, take my hand." And the boy took his dad's hand and they went into the house and shut the door, and they did not come out again until the morning. And they feasted upon the roasted lamb in the house. But they never sat down. They had their shoes on their feet, and they had their staff in their hand. And the little boy says, "Daddy, what is going to happen at twelve o'clock." The father says, "Every firstborn son that has not walked through a crimson archway and is partaking of the slain lamb will die at twelve o'clock." The little boy says, "Daddy, I am frightened. Will I die?" "No, son, you will not die." "Why will I not die?" "Because that little lamb has died for you. And although that little boy trembled when twelve o'clock came, praise God he did not die.

Many a time I have felt that I have had only a trembling faith in Jesus. It has been so weak, so imperfect, so poor, my faith in Jesus. But, praise God, if I am under the Crimson archway I am as safe as if I could sing a song. Even if I am weak I am still saved. Even if I tremble I am still saved. Even if I cannot really strongly believe, praise God, as long as I am under that Blood I am saved and safe for all eternity. Oh, there is power in the Blood, *It preserves the life.*

There was the cry at midnight. The firstborn son dies because there is no blood there, no protection there, no preservation there.

When you come to the great midnight hour will you be under the Blood? Tell me, my friend, when the clock strikes twelve in this world, will you be under the Crimson archway? Will you be ready when the call comes? Happy and blessed are those that are washed in the Blood of the Lamb. Friend, make sure you are under the Crimson archway tonight. Make sure you are under the Blood tonight. Make sure you are safe and saved for all eternity tonight.

THE BLOOD OF THE EVERLASTING COVENANT

I have one final thing to say to you. It was the Blood of the everlasting covenant. It was the Living Blood that brought Him from the tomb. Why? Away in Eternity God entered into a covenant with His Son. And He said, "My Son, if you go down to earth, if you bear the sins of my people, and carry them to the Cross, die for them in agony, and shed every drop of your life's Blood, I will make a covenant with you, I will make a solemn engagement with you, I will enter into a solemn contract with you that I will bring you from the dead. And everyone that believes in you shall not perish but have everlasting life."

The testament is of no strength while the testator liveth. When He died they took Him down from the Cross. Gentle hands washed His Body and laid spices and sweet-smelling myrrh upon it and wrapped it in a linen cloth and laid it in a virgin tomb (because it was a Virgin Body) where no one else had ever been laid. They rolled the great stone to the door and they turned their backs and went away. I hear a voice. What is that voice? It is a voice of Blood. Whose Blood is this? It is the voice of Jesus' Blood, and that voice says, "Father, I have fulfilled my engagements. Father, I have completed the contract. Father, the solemn bond that I entered into in Eternity, I have totally and absolutely fulfilled and completed. And the Blood said, "Raise Him from the dead. Bring Him forth in triumph. Put a crown upon His head. Put robes of glory about His Body. Set Him on the Everlasting Throne." And God, the Father, said, "I must heed this Precious Blood. It is the Blood of the Everlasting Covenant."

It was the Blood of Christ that cried for His release from the tomb. It was the Blood of Christ that pleaded with God that He should be resurrected. It was the Blood of Christ that stirred the charnel-house of death and brought Him forth in triumph. The God of peace brought again from the dead our Lord Jesus Christ, that Great Shepherd of the sheep through the Blood of the Everlasting Covenant.

THE SHATTERED COVENANT OF MEN

Let me show you another covenant. You will find it in the gospel of Matthew. And after He died, the religious world, and the political world, and the military world made a covenant. And the religious leaders came to Pontious Pilate. You read about in in Matthew. It is worth looking at. Matthew chapter twenty-seven and verse sixty-two, "Now the next day, that followed the day of the preparation, the chief priests and Pharisees came together unto Pilate, Saying, Sir, we remember that that deceiver said, while ye was yet alive, After three days I will rise again. Command, therefore, that the sepulchre be made sure until the third day, lest His disciples come by night, and steal Him away, and say unto the people, He is risen from the dead: so that last error shall be worse than the first. Pilate said unto them, Ye have a watch: go your way, make it as sure as you can."

Here was a contract between the religious leaders, the political leaders and the military leaders. "Make it as sure as you can." "Jesus in the tomb, keep Him there." And what did they do? They made the sepulchre sure. They sealed the stone, and they set a watch. There was a covenant between the religious, political and military world to keep Jesus in the tomb.

The Blood of Christ is more powerful than the religious world. The Blood of Christ is more powerful than the political world. The Blood of Christ is more powerful than the military world. And they all combined together. But the God of peace brought again our Lord Jesus Christ, that Great Shepherd of the sheep, through the Blood of the Everlasting Covenant. And the stone was rolled away, not to let Jesus out but to let them in to see that He was already gone. He rose through the granite wall. He rose through the graveclothes; they were lying there undisturbed.

THE MIRACLE OF THE RESURRECTION

People will tell you that the alabaster and the myrrh would harden so completely that you would need a hammer to break it. But Jesus needed no hammer to break the embalming of His Body. Why? Because the Blood is the life. He came forth through the Blood of the Everlasting Covenant. And one day, if Jesus comes not, this body of mine will be laid to rest, wrapped in the shroud, a lid on the coffin, laid in the tomb, and the worms will destroy it. But some day that body that is perished in the ground will hear the sound of the trumpet, and God will bring it forth. How? Through the Blood of the Everlasting Covenant. He not only promised that He would bring Jesus forth, but He promised that everyone of His people He would bring safely to Heaven. "Thine they were, Father; Thou gavest them me, and I have lost none of them. But I will raise them up at the last day." The resurrection to eternal life is sure to every man that leans on the Blood of Christ.

You can go home tonight and you can lay your head on your pillow; you do not need to worry, because, thank God, He will raise you up at the last day through the Blood of the Lamb.

Tell me, friend, is that Blood in your heart, or have you entered into a contract with evil to keep Him in the tomb? Are you part of the contract of Hell, or part of the covenant of Heaven? Please God that every man and woman in this meeting will be part of the covenant of Heaven. For Jesus' sake!

FOUR
THE VALUE OF THE BLOOD

THERE IS A GREAT rule or law in Biblical interpretation. It is called the law of the first mention. And if you turn over to Genesis chapter four and verse ten in your Bible, you will find there the first reference to the Blood in the Bible. The first Person to speak about blood in the Bible is God Himself. And he says to Cain, "The voice of thy brother's blood crieth unto me from the ground." That Old Testament passage has its New Testament exposition. You will find its New Testament exposition in Hebrews chapter twelve and in the verse twenty-four, "The Blood of sprinkling that speaketh better things than that of Abel." We have there the voice of the Blood.

Let me tell you something. There are four things in that first reference to the Blood that are important.

Firstly, the Blood has a voice. After death there is life, for the Blood speaks.
Secondly, the Blood has a loud voice. It cries; it cries to God.

Thirdly, the Blood has an effectual voice. God heard that Blood. God harkened to that Blood, and God heeded that Blood.

Fourthly, it cried from the place of the curse. "Thy brother's blood crieth unto me from the ground." And God said, "Cursed is the ground for thy sake, thorns will it bring forth." so from the place of the curse and the place of thorns, praise God the Blood speaks.

That is the voice of the Blood.

Yesterday morning I was speaking on The Virtue of the Blood. And we discovered another great law of Biblical interpretation. God teaches His people line by line, precept upon precept, here a little and there a little. The great doctrines of the Bible are not revealed all at once. They are revealed in a progressive way. First, there is the blade, then there is the ear, then there is the full corn in the ear.

SEVEN PICTURES OF THE LAMB

We discovered that the Virtue of the Blood has to do with Christ Who is the Lamb of God. In the Bible there is a sevenfold unveiling of the Lamb of God.

The first you will find in Genesis. We might just briefly refer to them as these will help us in our study this morning. You find the Provision of the Lamb in Genesis chapter twenty-two and verse eight. The question is asked by Isaac, "Where is the Lamb?"

We are at the foot of the hill. We are going up the mount of God. Young Isaac says, "Where is the Lamb?" and you will find that old Abraham says, "The Lord will provide a Lamb." There is *the Provision of the Lamb.*

Then when you turn over to Exodus chapter twelve you have *the Purity of the Lamb.* And you will notice that the Lamb was to be without blemish, it has to be taken out from among the herds - the goats and the cattle. It was a separate Lamb. It had to be kept for two periods of seven, a double perfection - fourteen days. It is a Lamb without blemish. The Purity of the Lamb.

Then if you turn to Isaiah chapter fifty-three you will find *the Person of the Lamb,* because it says, "He is led as a Lamb to the slaughter." (Isaiah 53: 7)

The Jewish people might have thought it was just a sacrificial lamb. But, no, it was to be a Person.

Then when you come to John's gospel chapter one and verse twenty-nine you read, "Behold the Lamb of God which taketh away the sin of the world." There you have *the Purpose of the Lamb.* He came to take away the sin of the world.

When we turn to I Peter chapter one and verse nineteen we find *the Preciousness of the Lamb*. The Lamb without blemish and without spot. The Precious Blood of Jesus. (We are going to come back to that this morning.)

Then, of course, in the Book of the Revelation, you remember in chapter five, no one could open the Book or loose the seven seals thereof. (We will be looking at that again this morning.)

Thank God for *the Potency of the Lamb*. He is able to take the Book and loose the seven seals thereof.

The last reference to the Lamb is a double reference. And the last chapter of Revelation tells us "the Throne of God and of the Lamb." Here we have *the Primacy of the Lamb*. He is first. The Lamb is all the glory in Emmanuel's Land!

So we have the virtue of the Blood. It is the Blood of the Lamb.

Then last night we were looking at the Vitality of the Blood. That great portion in Hebrew chapter thirteen and verse twenty, "Now the God of peace, that brought again from the dead our Lord Jesus through the Blood of the everlasting covenant." What was the power, what was the dynamic behind the empty tomb? None other than the Blood of the everlasting covenant that brought Him from the tomb!

We are going to look this morning, briefly, at The Value of the Blood, and tonight in the meeting we are going to look at The Victory of the Blood.

Let us come to this subject, The Value of the Blood. I want to take as my text, I Peter chapter one and verse nineteen, "Forasmuch as ye know that ye were not redeemed with corruptible things, as silver and gold, from your vain conversation received by tradition from your fathers (verse 18); But with the Precious Blood of Christ, as of a Lamb without blemish and without spot: Who verily foreordained before the foundation of the world, but was manifest in these last times for you."

Could I just say a word about the importance of the Blood of Christ. Ours is a Blood-stained Gospel. The Blood of Christ is the centre of that Gospel, but it flows in its mighty torrent right out to the circumference of the Gospel. The Blood of Christ is the pivot of God's plan of redemption, by which and around which all the purposes of God revolve. The Blood of Christ is the great heart of the Gospel revelation, but it throbs its crimson life to every part of the Body of Christ. To every believer there is given the power, and the efficacy, and the merit, and the availability, and the covering, and the cleansing, and the justification, and the sanctification and, praise God, one day the glorification of the Blood of Christ.

In God's eyes heaven is Blood-stained. In God's eyes earth is Blood-stained. In God's eyes the elect of God are Blood-stained. I come to a Blood-stained Throne. It was once a Throne of wrath. By the Blood, thank God, it is a mercy seat today where Jesus answers prayer, and I can humbly fall before His feet for none can perish there! A Blood-stained Throne. The church is Blood-stained. We sing today, with the multitude that no man can number, "We have washed our robes and made them white in the Blood of the Lamb." The church of Christ is Blood-stained. This Book is Blood-stained. Its every page, its every chapter, its every verse, is tinged with the Blood that flows from the open veins of Emmanuel. It is a Book stained with Blood. The path that we walk is a Blood-stained path. When I look down upon this path I am asked to travel, thank God I see the nail-prints of the Son of God. Jesus has gone before in this path, and He has left His Blood-prints upon it. And when I get to Heaven I am going to sing "Unto Him who loved me and loosed me from my sins." How? In His own most Precious Blood. To Him be the glory for ever and ever, Amen!

Having said that I want to come to the heart of my subject, the Value of the Blood.

I want to look first of all at the value of the Blood, *viewed eternally.* The Blood has an eternal value.

Then I want to look at the value of the Blood *biologically.* For biologically the Blood has a special value. It is different from any other blood that flowed in the veins of any other person. We are going to look at the value of the Blood biologically.

Then we are going to look at the value of the Blood *prophetically.* Because the Blood has prophetic value.

Then we are going to look at the value of the blood *potentially.* Praise God, there is power in the Blood of Christ. We believe it with all our hearts. Thank God this church believes in the Blood. No questions about it. Nobody comes up these pulpit stairs that doubts the value of the Blood of Christ. If anybody does ever come up these stairs and doubts the value of the Blood, you have my authority to throw him down the stairs. Let me tell you, friend, we have no question marks about the value of the Blood of Christ.

ONE: THE BLOOD OF CHRIST VIEWED ETERNALLY

Let us look at the Blood of Christ eternally, its eternal value.

Let us look at three scriptures very, very quickly. We have only time this morning to glance at this great subject.

First Corinthians chapter two, verses seven and eight, "But we speak the wisdom of God in a mystery, even the hidden wisdom, which God ordained before the world unto our glory, Which none of the princes of this world knew: for had they known it, they would not have crucified the Lord of glory." Now just mark those words, "before the world." That is eternity.

Turn to I Peter chapter one and verse nineteen, and we read of the precious Blood of Christ, of a Lamb Who verily was foreordained before the foundation of the world.

We have "before the world," "before the foundation of the world."

Then look at Revelation chapter thirteen and verse eight, and it says, "the Lamb slain from the foundation of the world." And the reference there is that when the foundation of the world was laid, He was already a Lamb slain.

So we have an eternal view of Christ slain from the foundation of the world. The Cross was rooted in the heart of God before it was set up on the hill crag called Golgotha. Before it was erected by the hands of men on Mount Calvary, the Cross was erected by the hands of God on the Hills of Eternal Glory. Let me say, the arms of the Cross embraced two eternities, and the top of the Cross reaches to the very ultimate Being of God Himself. What is this Cross? It is the outward demonstration in time what happened in eternity. It is the revelation of the heart of God. And when God's heart is revealed, it is revealed as a Bleeding heart.

Let us look at the vision of the Everlasting God. You will find that vision in Revelation chapter four. It is a powerful chapter. (We have not time to deal with this chapter this morning. But we can just glance at it.) Verse two, "And immediately I was in the spirit." And you need to be in the Spirit to see God. "Blessed are the pure in heart, for they shall see God." God give us the Blood-washing so that we will be pure in heart, so that we will see God. And do you know what it says here? It says, "And immediately I was in the spirit: and, behold, a throne was set in heaven, and One sat on the throne. And He that sat was to look upon like a jasper and a sardine stone, and there was a rainbow round about the throne, in sight like unto an emerald."

The ancient jasper stone was a transparent stone. It was a transparent stone that glittered and it sent forth all sort of beautiful colours. It is a type of the attributes of God. They are as clear as crystal, but they send forth various colours of His Omnipotence, Omniscience and His Omnipresence. I want you to notice something, that in the heart of the jasper stone there is set a sardine stone. That sardine stone, the ancients tell us, is the colour of blood. It was a blood-red stone.

When John, in the spirit, looked upon the One Who sat on the Throne, he saw the jasper of His attributes, he saw the many colours of God's great majesty. But right in the heart of the jasper there was set the blood-red sardine stone, because underlying all the attributes of God is God's everlasting purpose. What is that purpose? That purpose is to redeem us by the Blood of Christ, and make us fit inheritors of the Heaven of the saints of God and light.

So in the very Being of God in the vision that is given to John, there lies at the very heart of God the Blood of the Lamb. I tell you friend, this Blood has value for it lies in the very depths of the heart of God.

Before I had a reception of that Blood in my heart, God had the conception and inception of that Blood in His heart. Before I was able to grasp with my finite mind the fact that the Blood of Jesus Christ, God's Son, cleanseth me from all sin, God in His infinite mind planned my redemption, and He planned it by Blood alone. It is God's Word, God's Precious Word, it stands forever sure. "When I the Lord shall see the Blood, I will pass over you."

The Blood of Christ viewed eternally.

TWO: THE BLOOD OF CHRIST VIEWED PROPHETICALLY

Let us look at the Blood of Christ viewed prophetically.

The seedbed of all prophecy is the Book of Genesis. In Genesis you have the genesis of Blood in sacrificial atonement. If you study the Book of Genesis you will find that Genesis revolves around three great men, Adam - the father of the race, Noah - the father of the new world, Abraham - the father of the faithful. And you will discover three things if you look at these three great men. You will discover, number one, that there was a great epoch in the world's history happened in their day. A turning point in the world's history happened in their day. You will find that God gave to each of them a great promise, and that God added to that promise a special and peculiar sign.

ADAM

Look at Adam. It is not hard to tell what was the great epoch in Adam's life that changed the world. *It was the fall.* Adam fell. "By one man sin entered into the

world, and death by sin, so death passed upon all men, for that all have sinned."
What happened to Adam? What was that promise?

Turn to Genesis chapter three and verse fifteen, "The seed of the woman
shall bruise the serpent's head." But God gave Adam a sign. What was the sign? The
sign was the sign of the cheribum with the sword keeping the way to the tree of life.
The cheribum always denotes mercy in the Bible. The cheribum overshadowing
the mercy seat, it denotes always mercy. That sword, what does it denote? It
denotes justice. And you have mercy and justice and they keep the way to the tree
of life.

What must happen if I am gong to get to that tree of life? A sword must
penetrate my bosom, and I must die. And one dav the Blessed Son of God came
and bared His bosom to that sword. And, praise God, that flaming sword was
quenched in the Blood of the Lamb.

Do you know what the Queen uses her sword for? Either to strike the
aggressor or to elevate one of her subjects.

That sword that should have struck me into Hell, thank God instead He
touches me with it today and raises me to become a peer in the realm of Heaven,
to occupy the House of Lords, for we are kings with Him and we shall reign on the
earth.

How did this happen? It happened through the Blood of the Lamb.

The Blood of Christ has a value prophetically.

NOAH

Let us look at the second one, old Noah. What was the great epoch in his
day? *It was the flood.* What was the great promise given to Noah? The great promise
given to Noah, you will find it in Genesis chapter nine, that God would not destroy
the earth again with a flood. And what did God do? God gave a rainbow.

The rainbow has seven colours: red, orange and yellow. Of what are those
the colours? They are the colours of fire. You have seen the orange glow, the yellow
glow, the red glow of the fire. The other three colours are, of course, blue, purple
and indigo. And those three colours mingle together, the blue touches the yellow,
and when it touches the yellow you get green. And those are royal colours. The
royal colours they touch the colours of fire. So you have mercy and you have fire
touching and it becomes green.

We are told that if you are on an elevated site you can see the whole rainbow. Often, in an aeroplane, when the rainbow appears, you can see the complete circle.

Where was old Noah? He was up in Mount Ararat. He was well elevated. I believe that Noah saw the whole circle. And he discovered that the royal colours and the colours of fire came together, and they caused the colour green.

Go back to the Book of Revelation and you will find the fulfilment of that prophecy in Revelation chapter four. What does it say? It says, "And there was a rainbow round about the Throne, a sight like unto an emerald." (An emerald is green.) So the whole rainbow is now green. There are no royal colours. There are no fire colours. They are all green, because green speaks to me of everlasting perpetuity.

Thank God, we are the evergreens of God. There is no fading in the Father's love for us, in the Son's love or in the Spirit's love.

How did it come about? It came about by the mingling of the colours of fire with the colours of Heaven. How did that happen? Go back to Genesis and you will find that old Noah made an offering by blood. The last verse of chapter eight, he made an offering by blood unto the Lord.

I tell you today, there is a rainbow round about the Throne. And if you study that rainbow in Revelation chapter four you know what you will find? You will find that the saints of God sit inside the rainbow.

The four and twenty elders are a type of the church. Twelve from the Old Testament and twelve from the New. The complete church around the Throne, inside the rainbow.

Thank God we sit inside the circle that is brought about by the Blood of the Lamb.

The eternal value of the Blood viewed prophetically.

ABRAHAM

Could I just give you one last thought on old Abraham? What was the epoch in Abraham's life? *It was the call.* Genesis chapter twelve and verse one. If you look at the call, it resulted in the great promise of the covenant. There are seven things in that movement, It is a type of the everlasting covenant.

Look at Genesis chapter twelve and verse two, "I will make of thee a great nation." That is the first promise. "I will bless thee." That is the second one. "And make thy name great." That is the third one. "And thou shalt be a blessing." That is the fourth promise. "And I will bless them that bless thee." That is the fifth promise. "And curse him that curseth thee." That is the sixth. "And in thee shall all the families of the earth be blessed." That is the seventh promise.

You will notice those seven blessings come from the perfect call, and you have the number of completion. You have the three great "I wills." "I will bless thee," "I will bless them," "I will make of thee a great nation." "I will make of thee a great nation!" "I will bless thee!" "I will bless them!" The three "I wills." God the Father, God the Son, and God the Holy Ghost in the covenant of redemption.

What was the seal and sign of that covenant? The seal and sign of that covenant was, of course, circumcision. You will find that in Genesis chapter seventeen. And when God gave the covenant for circumcision to Abraham in chapter seventeen, God said, "I am going to change your name." And what did He do. He changed his name to Abram. Abram, four letters in the Hebrew. Abraham has five letters in the Hebrew. And God took the fifth letter "he" of the Hebrew alphabet and put it into the name Abraham.

My friend, five in scripture is the number of grace. And so we have grace. And how did it come about? It came about because of the circumcision, because of the circumcision of blood. Verse ten, Genesis chapter seventeen. "This is my covenant. Every man child among you shall be circumcised."

What does circumcision mean? We read over in Galatians chapter five what it means. Let us turn and have a look at it. It tells us there that if a person is circumcised, he is circumcised to keep the whole law. Galatians chapter five and verse three, "For I testify again to every man that is circumcised, that he is a debtor to do the whole law."

Christ was circumcised the eighth day. What did He do. The first time Christ shed His Blood, when did He shed it? He shed it at circumcision. He shed it on the eighth day, which is the day of resurrection. And you have in Christ's circumcision a preview of Calvary. He was a debtor to do the whole law.

The last time Christ shed His Blood was on the Cross. And what did He do at the Cross? He said, "Father, I have kept the whole law. I took myself a Blood obligation, when I was an infant of eight days, to do the whole law. I have fulfilled the whole law." And at the Cross He poured out His Blood a ransom for the many. Thank God the debt was fully paid. He became a debtor. He settled my debt. Thank God He has settled my debt for me!

Turn over to the Book of the Revelation chapter nineteen. Heaven is open, there is a Person on a white horse, and He has got a Name that no man can know.

And then it gives you the Name. It is called Logos - "The Word of God."

Here we have the five letters again, making up the name Logos. And you will notice He has that Name because His vesture is dipped in Blood.

The prophetic value of the Blood of Christ.

THREE: THE BLOOD OF CHRIST VIEWED BIOLOGICALLY

We want to look at the value of the Blood viewed biologically. This is a very important thing. The Blood of Christ physically speaking, biologically speaking, was different from any other blood.

There was never any blood like it before. There will never be any blood like it again.

Turn over to Genesis chapter two and you will find that God prepared for making this Blood. In Genesis chapter two and verse twenty-one, "And the Lord caused a deep sleep to fall upon Adam, and he slept: And He took one of His ribs, and closed up the flesh instead thereof. And the rib, which the Lord God had taken from the man, made He a woman, and brought her unto the man." And if you have a marginal Bible you will find a little number at the word "made". It is a reference to your margin. And the reference is "builded." God builded the woman. Why had God to take a special job and task in hand to build the woman? I will tell you why. He had to construct the woman in such a way that when she gave birth to a child, the blood-stream of the child did not come from the woman. The blood-stream owes its origin to the contribution of the male.

I asked a nurse one day for one of her books, and she gave me a copy of Gray's Anatomy, which is a recognised text book. And I noted in it that the foetal, that is the blood of the child, and maternal blood currents, do not intermingle, being separated from each other by the delicate walls of the villi. And never does the mother's blood give any contribution whatsoever to the blood of the child. So we owe the origin of our blood to our father, and not to our mother. God constructed woman so. Why? He knew there was a day coming that there was going to be a Virgin Birth; there was a day when God was going to do a biological miracle, and a woman was going to bear a Son and she was not going to bear Him in a natural manner, but in a supernatural manner.

Man came into the world in different ways. The first man came into the world by direct creation. That was a man without a woman or a man. Then woman came with a man without a woman, for she was taken out of the side. We came into the world by a man and a woman. Jesus Christ came into the world through the instrumentality of the woman alone. God did a supernatural work in Mary. And what happened? The Blood-stream owes its origin not to Mary but to the Holy Ghost. Conceived by the power of the Holy Ghost! Of one blood He has made every nation under earth. Every person in this meeting has a blood-stream poisoned with the cancer of sin. But, thank God, there is no sin in the Blood-stream of Jesus.

What was the result of this? I will tell you what the result was. (Mark these scriptures well.) Christ's Blood is innocent Blood as opposed to guilty blood. Matthew chapter twenty-seven and verse seven, "Judas said, I have betrayed innocent Blood."

There is not a man or woman in this meeting who has innocent blood. Thank God, Jesus Christ had Innocent Blood. Mark this with I Peter chapter one and verse nineteen, "Precious Blood." His Blood is precious Blood as opposed to corruptible blood. We are not redeemed with corruptible things, but with the Precious Blood." (1 Peter 1: 18) His Blood is Divine Blood as opposed to mere human blood. "The church of God which He purchased with His own Blood." Divine Blood as opposed to mere human blood. His Blood is Supernatural Blood as opposed to natural blood. "Neither by the blood of goats and calves, but by His own Blood He entered in once into the Holy Place, having obtained eternal redemption for us. (Hebrews 9:12.) His Blood is voluntarily-shed Blood opposed to accidentally-spilled blood. John chapter ten and verse eighteen, "No man taketh it from me." "My Blood which is shed for many for the remission of sins." His Blood is Cleansing Blood as opposed to congealed blood. "The Blood of Jesus Christ His Son keeps on cleansing from all sin." His Blood is Living Blood as opposed to lost blood. "Brought again from the dead our Lord Jesus Christ, that great Shepherd of the sheep, through the Blood of the everlasting covenant." His Blood is peace-speaking Blood as opposed to enmity-arousing blood. "The Blood of sprinkling that speaketh better things than that of Abel." His Blood is justifying Blood as opposed to the blood of judgment. "Justified freely by His Blood." (Romans 5: 9)

That is what happened, let us view the Blood of Christ biologically. It is different from any other blood. That is why it has value.

What was it the old Puritan, Stephen Charnock, said? He said, "At the Blood-stream from the Cross there flows all the attributes of God in solution." Yes! What are the attributes of God? God is a Spirit, Infinite. There is Infinity in the Blood of Christ. It is Infinite Blood. Eternal, Unchangeable, in its Being. Thank God the Blood of Christ is Infinite, Eternal, Unchangeable in its Being. "Wisdom," there is

Wisdom in the Blood. "Power," there is power in the Blood. "Justice," "Goodness and Truth," all in the Blood of Christ.

The Blood can save you forever. It can find you stained, and soiled, and fit for Hell, a child of wrath, a child of woe, a child of Hell, but touch a child of wrath, touch a child of the Devil, touch a child of woe with the Blood and suddenly, miraculously, supernaturally, wonderfully, and, praise God, eternally he becomes a Son of God. It is only the Blood of Christ can do that. That is the Blood of the Lamb. That is what we are talking about.

FOUR: THE BLOOD OF CHRIST VIEWED POTENTIALLY

Of course, lastly, we can view the Blood of Christ potentially. Turn over to Revelation chapter five. It was the Blood that opened the Book. It is powerful to open the Book. "And John wept, and one of the elders saith unto him, Weep not: behold the lion of the Tribe of Judah, the Root of David, hath prevailed. And I beheld, and, lo, in the midst of the throne there stood a Lamb as it had been slain." In the original it is "A newly-slain Lamb in the midst of the Throne." There stood a Lamb as it had been slain, a newly-slain Lamb.

The Body of Christ was incorruptible. It lay in the grave but it saw no corruption. The Blood of Christ is incorruptible. It did not see any corruption either. The Blood of Christ never went back into the veins of Jesus, because flesh and blood cannot inherit eternal life or inherit the kingdom of God. Our bodies in Heaven will be made of flesh, bones and spirit. There will be no blood in them. "Handle me and see, a spirit hath not flesh and blood." No! "A spirit hath not flesh and bones as ye see me to have."

What happened to the Blood of Christ? The Blood of Christ had the same resurrection as the body of Christ. And Jesus Christ took that Blood, and what was that Blood? It was His life. It was all that He did on earth, and it was all that He offered to God on the Cross. And He took that Blood, according to Hebrews chapter nine, and in Hebrews chapter nine you will find what He did with it. (Hebrews 9; 12) "Neither by the blood of goats or calves, but by His own Blood He entered into the Holy Place, having obtained eternal redemption for us."

As the high priest took the blood on the day of atonement and parted the veil, and sprinkled the mercy seat, so Jesus Christ in the glory of His resurrection took His own Blood with Him. And He presented it at the Father's Throne. The Blood is there before and on the Throne. "His own wounds in Heaven declare His work on earth is done."

Look at verse twenty-four in Hebrews chapter nine, "For Christ is not entered into the holy places made with hands, which are the figures of the true, but into heaven itself, now to appear in the presence of God for us." He has entered in. How did He enter in? With His own Blood. It was necessary that He not only should die on the brazen altar, it was necessary that He should present His Blood at God's Everlasting Throne.

TWO IMPORTANT FACTS

There are two things in the Blood. There is the shedding of the Blood and there is the sprinkling of the Blood. He has done them both. Thank God He shed His Blood at Calvary. Thank God, He sprinkled the Blood at God's right hand. Thank God, there is a golden bell ringing today on the garment of the Great High Priest, and that golden bell is surrounded by the pomegranates on the border of His garment. And the border, the hen of His garment, speaks of the finished work, for the music comes from the finished work of Christ. Thank God, we can say like the Psalmist, "Happy are the people that hear the joyful sound." We have heard the joyful sound this morning, have we not? There is power in the Blood of Christ. Yes!

The Blood of Christ has not only opened the Book, it has opened Heaven. That is what the Blood has done. The value of the Blood, viewed potentially, has opened Heaven. "Having boldness therefore brethren to enter in by the Blood of Jesus, by a new and living way."

If you get the hold of this truth it will revolutionise your prayer life. You are going to plead with God by a new and living way, by the Blood of Christ.

One final thing, you can view the value of the Blood, it opens the grave.

The first three references give you a basic idea of the Blood, and the basic idea of the Blood in scripture is not death but life. "Thy brother's blood crieth to me from the ground." But he was already dead. Here is life after death. "He being dead yet speaketh."

Thank God the Blood gives me the promise of life after death. I will die, if Jesus tarries, but, praise God, there is life for me beyond the tomb.

Then in the ninth chapter of Genesis we read, "The blood is life." So we discover that the Blood not only gives us the promise of life after death, but the Blood gives us the promise of the life that now is. I can live victoriously now. Why? By the Blood of Christ. "Now by this I overcome, nothing but the Blood of Jesus." I have the promise of the life that now is.

Something else. The third reference to the Blood is in Exodus chapter twelve. (I was talking about it last night.) There is life preserved. It is a wonderful statement about the Blood there it occurs nowhere else in the Bible. Exodus chapter twelve; it says you must strike the Blood on the doorposts and on the lintel of the door.

I am glad today that God struck a way into Heaven for me through the Blood of the Lamb. He opened a door for me to eternal safety. He made a Crimson archway. Thank God I can walk under that archway.

When I went home last night I was talking to my firstborn son. I said, "Kyle, have you gone under the archway. Are you sheltered under the Blood?" He says "Yes, daddy, I have gone in under the archway."

What happens if you are under the archway? The firstborn lives, for God says, "I will stand guard over you." The life preserved!

The Blood opens the grave. And some day we will fall asleep in Jesus. Some day our bodies will rest in the dust. Some day a trumpet will sound. There will be a strange stirring in the tomb. We will rise and we will be changed, transformed, and we will meet the Lord in the air. Why? Because we will be singing, "Washed in the Blood of the Lamb."

"Who, who are these
Beside the chilly wave?
Just on the borders of the silent grave,
Shouting Jesus' power to save,
'Washed in the Blood of the Lamb'?"

Thank God for every one of us who knows the value of the Blood applied to our hearts. May we know it today in this house.

For Jesus' sake.

FIVE
THE VICTORY OF THE BLOOD

TURN TO THE BOOK OF the Revelation chapter twelve. This tells of a great battle which is going on. Oh, there is a great battle on all right. No doubt about that, we are in the midst of that conflict, in the midst of that confrontation, in the midst of that war.

Now in verse eleven we have a word here, "and they overcame him." Who was that "him"? Look at verse nine - you have a word here - "The great dragon was cast out, that old serpent called the Devil and Satan." That is who the enemy is. "And they overcame him." Who did they overcome? they overcame the dragon; they overcame the serpent!

I want you to notice there are two animal representations there. There is the dragon and there is the serpent. And there are two names of the Devil given - the Devil and Satan. And he is likened to a dragon and a serpent. And it says, "They overcame him by the Blood of the Lamb." By the Blood of the Lamb! They overcame who? The dragon, the serpent, that old serpent the Devil and Satan. "They overcame him by the Blood of the Lamb, and by the word of their testimony, and they loved not their lives unto the death."

ALL OPPOSITION TO THE CHURCH SATANIC

In all the seasons of the church's testimony for God on earth, there has been satanic opposition to the work of the church. Behind everything that opposes the word of the church lies the terror of the dragon, the subtlety of the serpent, the power of the Devil and the opposition of Satan. He is there opposing, resisting the work of the church.

We find also in this chapter that the saints are engaged in the battle with the Devil. The saints of God have to fight. They do not sit in armchairs and put up their feet and watch the television. No! They are engaged in a fight. There is a battle on. It is a life or death struggle, because the Devil is filled with satanic malignity against the church. Oh, he hates the church!

If the Devil could smash the Free Presbyterian Church he would do it. He is fighting to smash it. We want to pray for every minister. You know if every member of the Free Presbyterian Church fell into sin it would be very sad, it would be a great tragedy, but it would not affect the ministry of the church so very much. But what if Ian Paisley fell into sin, what if Ian Paisley got into some immoral entanglement with some woman, what if Ian Paisley took money that did not belong to him, what if Ian Paisley did something that brought dishonour to Christ? Would not the Devil laugh? Would not the Devil be glad if he could do that with some minister of the Church.

It is not the first time that has happened to some minister. It is not the first time a leader of a church has been smashed, smashed by the Devil.

Man, would not the Devil glow? Would not the old apostates laugh and say to you Free Presbyterians, "There are your leaders. There are your ministers. There is your man of God." I tell you, friend, we are in a fight. The Devil would like to get us out of the battle, would he not? The Devil would like to put a smear on our testimony. The Devil would like to find something that they could point a finger at. Oh but, praise God, we are going to get victory over the Devil. The Devil is not going to smash up the church. Oh, he has some malicious plans, some nice malignant plans, laid for us, but, praise God, we are going to overcome. I am glad there is power in the Blood to deal with the malignity of the Devil.

THE CRAFT OF THE DEVIL

Then, of course, the Devil is very crafty. He has been destroying churches since he came down to this earth, since the church started away back in Eden's garden. (You may not agree with that, but if you know the Scripture you would know that was right!) Let me just tell you this, he has been opposing the church ever since there was a godly man on earth.

The first man who was a fundamentalist, who was he? They called him Abel. He did not build an altar of man's device like Cain. He built a plain altar, put a sacrifice on it, believed in the Blood. What did Cain do? He killed him. There you have the craft of the Devil to destroy the testimony of a person that stands for the fundamentals of the gospel. Oh, the Devil is crafty.

You know, some years ago two men visited me, and they said, "Mr. Paisley, you are a great preacher." When a persons says that to you, watch him. He always flatters you before he puts the knife into your back. So I did not say anything. Then they said to me, "We are very afraid for your wife and family." I said, "I am very glad to know that you are both concerned about my family. It is very nice of you." They said, "We feel that if you just preached the gospel and left off Popery and the World Council of Churches, and you did not say the outrageous things you say, you would have a great church, and God would bless you mightily." So I just opened the door of the room they were in, and I said, "If you two fellows do not go through that door it will give me the greatest of pleasure to assist you to go through that door. You came here from the Devil. You spoke as the Devil. I cannot cast the Devil out of you, but it will give me great pleasure to cast the Devil and you out as well." Yes! I want to tell you, that is the craft of the Devil.

How many ministers started on fire for God, and when their church built up, then they wanted to be respectable. "I would like to get an invitation to sit on the ministerial council. I would like my brother ministers to put their hand out and shake hands with me."

I never get any invitations to sit on the ministers' council. They have one in East Belfast. They never send me an invitation, or else the postman tears them up and I do not get them! They never come! You know why? You will have no difficulty if you stand right up and down the line for God. You will have no difficulty. Of course, if you are a pussyfooter, a fence sitter, a cream puff preacher, a soft peddler, you will get the invitations. But if you are the man of God standing for God you will not desire those invitations.

THE ACCUSATIONS OF THE DEVIL

The Devil is crafty!

The Devil also is the accuser of the brethren. And there are some people mighty good at doing the Devil's work. I tell you, there are some Christians the Devil has as special agents and they accuse the brethren.

I used to think it was my duty to reconcile church members. I had two women and they fought. And I thought, as a young pastor, I could settle them. What a fool I was. Man, I know now to never get in between two fighting women. They will stop fighting one another and they will fight you. And that is exactly what happened. I got these two women together and I said, "Now you are both Christians; you should not be carrying on like this." And they started on me. I am telling you they nearly got their finger nails into me before the end of the meeting. I never did that again. But I found out a better thing to do. If anyone comes to me and says, "I have something against another Christian." I say, "Write it down and put your name at it." And do you know what I find? I find that people who are so quick to give an accusation, they back away. I say, "Use the pen now, get it down, get your signature at it." They say, "Oh now, Mr. Paisley, I would not like to write it down." If you cannot write it down, shut up!

The Devil is an accuser of the brethren.

If I believed everything that people tell me that Willie McCrea said about me, I would not speak to him. If he believed everything they say that I said about him, he would not be speaking to me. But it is a pack of lies. For if we have anything to say about one another we are straight and plain. We can say it face to face.

This is what the Devil does. He would like the ministers of the Free Presbyterians to be at sixes and sevens. He would like the Committee of the church to be at sixes and sevens and the Sunday School teachers. Some old person with their tongue wagging at both ends, what harm they can do to the church of Jesus Christ.

The Devil is the accuser of the brethren. You know what happens? He accuses them day and night before God, that is what he does. Oh, I thank God, they overcame him by the Blood of the Lamb. Thank God the accusations of the Devil stop when you plead the Blood of Christ, thank God we can face the accusations of the Devil, and triumph gloriously in the Name of Jesus.

Now I must start to preach. That is only the introduction to my sermon. I was just saying some things by the way!

THEIR WEAPONS - THE BLOOD OF THE LAMB AND THE WORD OF TESTIMONY

Let us look at the test, "They overcame him by the Blood of the Lamb, and by the word of their testimony."

I want you to notice their weapons - "The Blood of the Lamb, the word of their testimony."

You know friend, the greatest example of the defeat of the Devil was when the Lord triumphed over the Devil.

I was thinking today in my meditation on this sermon, of the day when the Lord was led by the Spirit into the wilderness. Do you remember that? Do you remember the Devil came to defeat Him in the wilderness? He came to bring Him down. And he tempted Him in three ways. The Devil's temptations all come in three ways: the world, the flesh and the Devil. He tempted Him in the realm of the flesh - "Make these stones bread." He tempted Him in the realm of the world: "Fall down and all these kingdoms shall be yours." He tempted Him as the Devil and said, "Cast yourself down and people will worship you." The world, the flesh and the Devil, that is the three realms along which the Devil always attacks.

How did the Lord defeat the Devil? He defeated him by the Word of His testimony. He opened up the Book. What Book? The Book of Deuteronomy. You know, the old Devil is sore about that to this day. There is no book that the modernists more attack than the Book of Deuteronomy. Why? The Lord gave the old Devil such a hiding with that Book, he is still licking his wounds to this day. And that is why all his emissaries are all against the Book of Deuteronomy. When I hear an old modernist minister saying, "I do not like the Book of Deuteronomy," I say,

"You are a child of the Devil." The Lord tanned the Devil's hide with that Book, in the wilderness. By the Word of His testimony!

Ah, but there was a second time the Devil attacked Jesus. The Devil met Jesus in the garden of Gethsemane. What to do? To kill Him. Why did the Devil want to kill Jesus in the garden of Gethsemane? The Devil knew that if Jesus got to the Cross, he was finished. And if you read the life of Christ you will notice that the Devil wanted to kill Jesus over and over again before He got to the Cross. Even before He was born he whispered into the ear of Joseph. He said, "Mary, your wife, she is an adulteress. Get her stoned according to the Mosaic law." Why did the Devil whisper that in Joseph's ear? He wanted to kill Jesus before He was born. He wanted to destroy Him before He could get out to the Cross. But the Holy Ghost said, "Fear not to take unto thyself Mary, thy wife, for that which is conceived in her is of the Holy Spirit." All through His life the Devil was attacking Jesus.

The greatest attack that the Devil ever put up against the Lord Jesus, from the day of His temptation to the Cross, was at the garden of Gethsemane.

I want you to turn over to Luke's gospel chapter twenty-two, and I want you to keep your finger on that portion. Luke 22: 41, "And He was withdrawn from them about a stone's cast, and kneeled down, and prayed, saying, "Father, if Thou be willing, remove this cup from me: nevertheless, not my will, but Thine, be done. And there appeared an angel unto Him from heaven, strengthening Him." Now just keep your finger on that passage and turn over to Hebrews chapter five and you will get the commentary on that passage. Hebrews 5: 7, "Who in the days of His flesh, when He had offered up prayers and supplications with strong crying and tears unto Him that was able to save Him from death, and was heard in that He feared."

In the garden of Gethsemane the Devil came to kill Jesus. And He cried to God to save Him from death. And He cried with strong crying and tears. So great was the satanic influence in Gethsemane's garden that the disciples slept. They could not keep their eyes open. The old Devil made them heavy with sleep. Jesus Christ is there. It was not the angel that defeated the Devil. I want to show you something that I noticed today. After the angel had left Him what happened? "And being in agony He prayed more earnestly: and His sweat was as it were great drops of Blood falling down to the ground." I want to tell you, once His body was crimson with His Blood He overcame the Devil.

How did He overcome the Devil in the wilderness temptation. By the Word of His testimony. How did He overcome the Devil in Gethsemane's garden? By His

Blood. When the Blood appeared the Devil fled from Him. The Devil could not fight Him in the crimson garment of His Precious Blood. There is power, Devil-defeating power in the Blood of the Lamb. The Lord Jesus is the great example. He overcame the Devil by the Word of His testimony, and by the Blood of the Lamb.

That is how we are going to overcome the Devil.

Of course, I want to show you the glory of overcoming. It is a great thing to overcome the old Devil, and to see him overthrown.

If you turn to the Book of the Revelation you will find there are seven letters written to seven churches. And at the end of every letter he tells us about the overcomers. Yes! They overcame him by the Blood of the Lamb.

You will notice that every blessing to the overcomer is victory over the Devil's works. "For this purpose was the Son of God manifested that He might destroy the works of the Devil.

ONE, VICTORY OVER THE CURSE

Turn to the first promise to the overcomer. You will find it in Revelation chapter two and verse seven. Mark it in your Bible; keep it in mind. "To him that overcometh I will give to eat of the tree of life, which is in the midst of the paradise of God." "They overcame Him by the Blood of the Lamb."

What keeps us from the tree of life? The curse. Who brought in the curse? The Devil, when he seduced Eve and Eve fell and Adam sinned.

Praise God, him that overcometh, he is not barred from the tree of life. Thank God, the man that overcomes, he gets right to the tree of life. And the fruit that is forbidden to others, praise God it is given to the person that overcomes by the Blood of the Lamb. We are going to get there!

Every time these words are mentioned in these overcoming passages, and the blessings to the overcomer, there is a comment further on in the Book of Revelation.

If you want the comment on Revelation chapter two and verse seven, turn to Revelation chapter twenty-two and verse two, "In the midst of the street of it, and on either side of the river, there was the tree of life, which bare twelve manner of fruits, and yielded her fruit every month." Verse fourteen of Revelation chapter twenty-two, "Blessed are they that do His commandments, that they may have right to the tree of life, and may enter in through the gates into the city." "Sweeping through the gates of the new Jerusalem, singing, Washed in the Blood of the Lamb."

They overcame him. How? By the Blood of the Lamb. Where did they get to? They got to the tree of life in the midst of the paradise of God.

TWO, VICTORY OVER DEATH

Come to the second one. Revelation chapter two and verse eleven.

The first overcoming overcomes the curse. The second overcoming overcomes death. Verse eleven of Revelation chapter two, "He that overcometh shall not be hurt of the second death."

What is the second death? Turn to the commentary later on in the Book. Revelation chapter twenty and verse fourteen, "And death and hell were cast into the lake of fire. This is the second death." Revelation chapter twenty-one and verse eight, "But the fearful, and unbelieving, and the abominable, and murderers, and whoremongers, and sorcerers, and idolaters, and all liars, shall have their part in the lake which burneth with fire and brimstone: which is the second death." "He that overcometh shall not be hurt of the second death."

Do you know, the purpose of the Devil is to drag you down to hell. That is his purpose. But, thank God, we can overcome by the Blood of the Lamb.

I have got a body out of the grave tonight. I have got a soul out of hell. I will never burn in the pit, Hallelujah! Why? Because of the Blood of the Lamb. He has paid it all. He has satisfied Divine Justice. Like C.H. Spurgeon, we can say, "With one tremendous draft He drank damnation dry for me." Thank God, there is power in the Blood of Christ. Victory over Hell. Brother, you will never be there! Sister, you will never be there! The Devil planned it. He purposed it. He designed it. He devised it. He has done everything in his satanic power to drag me to Hell. But, praise God, I am saved from Hell, and I am saved by the Blood of the Lamb. "They overcame him by the Blood of the Lamb." Saved from the curse by the Blood! Saved from Hell by the Blood! There is victory in the Blood of Christ, is there not?

THREE, VICTORY OVER THE LAW

Let us come to verse seventeen. There is the next overcomer. Revelation chapter two and verse seventeen. "To him that overcometh will I give to eat of the hidden manna, and will give him a white stone, and in the stone a new name written, which no man knoweth saving he that received it." There is victory over the law.

You say, "How do you get that? Oh, my friend, you compare spiritual things with spiritual. What was in the mercy seat? I will tell you what was in the mercy seat. There was a pot of manna in the mercy seat. There was a stone that was written on by the hand of God. The tables of stone! There was the vindication of a man's name in the ark of the covenant, underneath the mercy seat in Aaron's rod which budded. Those things were there.

When people looked in the ark, they took the lid off and looked in! they were stricken. But, praise God, today I can look into the ark, and I can see the hidden manna; I can see the white stone written with the hand of God. And, praise God, my name is written there. I am an Aaron; I have been vindicated; my rod has blossomed, budded, and brought forth and I have victory over the law. How? By the Blood of Christ. Let me tell you, friend. The law has nothing to say to me in retribution or judgment. The law has everything to say to me in blessing and in salvation. The law cursed me because I have sinned. The law pronounces me not guilty because Jesus died for me, I have access to the ark and I can see the hidden manna.

You could compare this to Revelation chapter fourteen and verse one, the new name that is written. Just look at that, and I do not want you to miss it. "And I looked, and, lo, a Lamb stood on the mount Sion, and with Him an hundred and forty and four thousand (those are not Jehovah's Witnesses, by the way; those are the saved people), having His Father's Name written in their foreheads." We have the Father's Name in our foreheads. Praise God for that.

Victory over the law!

FOUR, VICTORY OVER THE WORLD

Then look at this one in verse twenty-six of Revelation chapter two, "victory over the nations." "And he that overcometh, and keepeth my works unto the end, to him will I give power over nations: And he shall rule them with a rod of iron; as the vessels of a potter shall they be broken in shivers: even as I received of my Father." Victory over the world! And you know what the comment on that one is? Turn over to the chapter that we read, chapter twelve and verse five, "And she brought forth a man child, Who was to rule all nations with a rod of iron: and the child was caught up unto God, and to His Throne."

Christ conquered the world. "They overcome him (the Devil) by the Blood of the Lamb." And, thank God, we are going to conquer the world with the Lord Jesus Christ.

I want to tell you something. When you get seven in the Bible, always look carefully at the fourth one. There is always something good about the fourth one. Because when you have seven in the Bible, the fourth is the middle one. There is the three to one side and there is the three to the other side. The fourth one is the middle one. Mark it, there is a special thing about this fourth one. Revelation 2: 28, "And I will give him the Morning Star." It is not in any of the others. That is the fourth one. You know why? Because in the centre of it all is Jesus Himself. Praise His Wonderful Name!

Do you want the comment on that? Turn to the last chapter of the Book of the Revelation and you will find who the Morning Star is. He is the Root and offspring of David, and the Bright and Morning Star. Who is he? My Jesus. It is Jesus Himself.

Oh, there are blessings for the overcomer. What is the main blessing the Blood brings to you? Christ Himself, that is the central blessing, is it not? "I will give him the Bright and Morning Star."

FIVE, VICTORY OVER SIN

We come now to the fifth one. We will find that the fifth one is "He that overcometh, the same shall be clothed in white rainment; and I will not blot out his name out of the Book of life, but I will confess his name before my Father, and before His angels." (Rev. 3: 5).

The commentary on that is found in Revelation chapter seven and verse thirteen. And the question is asked: "What are these which are arrayed in white robes? and whence came they? And I said unto him, Sir, thou knowest. And he said to me, These are they which came out of great tribulation, and have washed their robes."

Victory over sin. Hallelujah! Sin is the offspring of Satan. Praise God, He is going to give us a white robe. There is victory over sin.

My old father, used to always start off this Easter Convention with the first message every Easter Monday. He would say, "I am wearing the same suit as the day I was saved." Yes! What did he mean? The day God saved us He gave us a suit. It is as white as the driven snow. Thank God, we are still wearing it. We are going to wear it in Heaven for all Eternity. There is not a spot on it. It is an immaculate Blood-washed suit of the saints of God. Tailor-made! I am telling you it fits us ideally. It is just for me. It covers all my sin!

What does it say? How do you overcome? By the Blood of the Lamb. That is how you overcome.

SIX, VICTORY OVER LIFE'S PILGRIMAGE

The next one you will find in verse twelve. "Him that overcometh will I make a pillar in the temple of my God, and he shall go no more out: and I will write upon him the Name of my God, and the name of the city of my God, which is new Jerusalem which cometh down out of heaven from my God: and I will write upon him my new name."

Turn to Revelation chapter thirteen and verse eight, "And all that dwell upon the earth shall worship him, whose names are not written in the book of life of the Lamb slain from the foundation of the world." Turn to chapter twenty and verse fifteen, "And whosoever was not found written in the book of life was cast into the lake of fire."

Thank God our name is not going to be blotted out, not going to be blotted out of the book of life.

Let me show you verse twelve of Revelation chapter three, "Him that overcometh will I make a pillar in the temple."

I was looking at that verse. What is that victory over? That is victory over life's pilgrimage. What am I doing? I am going in and out. Would I not like to be a pillar tonight in the temple of our God.

When we come to an Easter Convention like this, would you not like to stay on the mountain top? Never go home. Just stay and worship God. One day we are going to have an Easter Convention for all eternity. We are going to celebrate the resurrection of Christ for all eternity. I want to tell you, I am going to be able to sing then. And I tell you something, I never took a music lesson in my life upon a harp, but I will out harp you in Heaven. I will indeed; I know some people who harp on so much that they would out harp you on earth, but I am going to out harp you all in Heaven. What a day, when you get that golden harp, brother! You will really play that harp! Yes!

You know when they stand yonder on the sea of glass, everything is filled with clarity in Heaven. There are no black spots in Heaven. The sea of glass, clear as crystal. We are going to lift up those golden harps and we are going to gaze upon the Lamb Who is all the glory in Emmanuel's Land. Our hearts are going to be filled with that love that we could never inspire on earth, because we have been limited by the fleshly limitations of time. And our whole body, soul and spirit will come into the everlasting ambit of Heaven's everlasting day. I tell you, we will sing about Jesus as we would have longed to have done on earth, but we could not have done it. He is going to make us a pillar in the temple of our God.. We are going to remain there and He is going to write on that pillar. He is going to write on that pillar the name of the city of our God. And He is going to write upon it the Name of our God. He is going to write upon it our new name.

How are we going to get there? By the Blood of the Lamb. That is how we are going to get there. Will that not be a great day?

At times I sit in my study and I close my eyes and think about Heaven. It is going to be a great day. When we all get to heaven, what a day of rejoicing that will be! When we all see Jesus, we will sing and shout the victory!

I have a few people I want to look up in Heaven when I get there. I want to meet old Martin Luther and have a yarn with him, about how he fought the Pope in his day. I want to tell him we had his thesis on the door of the Martyrs Memorial, and say, "Martin, you ought to have been down yonder. We had your thesis on the door, against the Pope." Martin will say, "Praise God, Ian, there is no Pope here. We are in a place where there is no Pope here." Is that not right? Amen! We believe it. Sure! We are going to talk.

I think there is one person I really want to see in Heaven after I have seen Jesus. Do you know who it is? The dying thief. I like that dying thief. He is the only person who spoke a word for Jesus when He was dying. The disciples ran away. The women stood afar off. Mary's heart was broken and she was speechless. But the old dying thief spoke a good word about Jesus. I want to take that dying thief by the hand and say to him, "You spoke a good word about my Saviour as He hung on the Cross." I want to put my arms round him and tell him I love him; he is a brother in Christ; he spoke a good word about Jesus.

You show me a man, whether he be in Australia, or New Zealand, or Africa, or America, or in Europe, that is speaking a good word about Jesus, he is my friend, a friend of the fundamentalists of the world, the people that are speaking a good word about Jesus. I want to be with that crowd. That is my crowd. That is the crowd I want to run with. That is the crowd I want to be labelled with, and catalogued with, and put away with, the crowd that speaks well about Jesus.

We are never going to leave Heaven. We will be there forever. You are going to work you know. You are not going to put your feet up and laze about. Our God is going to have things for us to do. His servants will serve Him.

I was reading C.H. Spurgeon the other day. Spurgeon says that there are creations beyond this creation, filled with creatures God has made, who have never sinned. I am going to be sent on a mission to those far-off planets and tell them the wonder of what Jesus did for poor lost sinners.

Now, I am not saying that is right. But, mind you, if Spurgeon thought that, he was a clever fellow; he might not be far off the mark.

I am going to serve the Lord in Heaven. I am going to serve Him. And you know some day the Lord is going to take over this earth. "The kingdoms of this world shall become the kingdoms of our Lord and of His Christ." I can assure you of that! Yes! We are going to serve Him. We will serve Him without sin.

If there is one thing that hinders me in my service for God, that thing is sin. Praise God, we will have overcome in eternity. We will never go out again. That meeting will never have a doxology. They will never say "Amen," and dismiss the congregation. We will be there forever. Oh, what a day that is going to be.

We have had a sweet taste of Heaven today in this Church. I think God has come down our souls to greet, and glory has crowned the mercy seat. But, praise God, Heaven is never going to end.

When I was a boy in Sunday School, my mother, at the Sunday School used to get all the children together at the end of the annual meeting, and she used to make them stand up round the Communion Table and sing a little hymn.

"Our friends on earth we meet with pleasure,
How swift the moments fly,
But ever comes the thought of parting,
That we must say goodbye.
We will never say goodbye in Heaven.
For in that Land of joy and song,
Thank God they never say goodbye."

Why? They overcame Him by the Blood of the Lamb.

SEVEN, VICTORY OVER ALL THINGS

One last one. It is in Revelation three and verse twenty-one "To him that overcometh will I grant to sit with me in my Throne, even as I also overcame, and am set down with my Father in His Throne." That is victory over all things. Oh, yes, we have reached the Throne. Lord, who is that sitting beside you on the Throne? Who is he? "That is a poor, guilty, vile, lost, hell-deserving sinner. That is a man that should have gone to Hell. That is a man that raked in the kennels of sin, in the hovels of the damned. But one day My grace reached him. One day My Blood washed him. One day My Spirit regenerated him. One day I took him from a fearful pit and from the miry clay, and on a Rock I set his feet establishing his way!" "Lord, what have you done with him?" "I have made him an overcomer. I have given him the power of the Blood of Christ. The virtue of this Blood is his. The voice of this Blood is his. The victory of this Blood is his. And it has raised him." "Where?" "To sit with Jesus on the throne."

Will I ever sit there with Jesus? Yes, I will sit there with Jesus if I overcome. That is what the Free Presbyterian Church needs to be. A company of overcomers. That is what we need to be. If I overcome the Devil I will sit with Him. I am going to sit down with Jesus.

What a day that will be when I sit down with Him. I think I will look down at His feet, and I will say, "Lord, there is a nail-print there." And He will say, "Yes, Ian, I bore it for you." "Lord Jesus, there are thorn marks in your brow. And there is a scar on your side." "Yes, Ian, I bore it for you." And He will hold my hand, and say, "Ian, it was well worth while." And I will say, "Saviour, it could not have been, for a filthy old sinner like me." And He will say, "Listen, Who for the joy that was set before Him, endured the Cross, despising the shame, and is set down with the Father in Glory." He will say, "It was well worth while." I will say, "Lord Jesus, I did not serve you the way I should. I did not stand for you the way I ought. I could have fought harder. I could have prayed harder. I could have preached harder. I could have laboured harder." And He will say, "I know the flesh was weak, but the spirit was willing. And remember, you are not here because you worked your passage. You are here because of the Blood of the Lamb."

> *"The Bride eyes not her garment,*
> *But her dear Bridegroom's face,*
> *I will not gaze on Glory,*
> *But on the King of grace,*
> *Not at the crown He gifteth,*
> *But on His pierced hand,*
> *The Lamb is all the Glory*
> *In Emmanuel's Land."*

"Oh, I am my Beloved's,
And my Beloved is mine:
He brings a poor vile sinner
Into His house of wine.
I stand upon His merit,
I know no safer stand,
Not even where Glory dwelleth,
In Emmanuel's Land."

Praise God for the Blood of Christ! Let us preach it. Let us exalt it. Let us wash in it. Let us know its life-giving, energising power. Let us know its Devil-defeating efficacy. Let us know its incorruptible liquidity. Let us know its tremendous merit, and its eternal virtue. Above all, let us experience its overcoming potency. And may everyone of us be overcomers.

For Jesus' Sake.

Amen and Amen

4 Joseph:
a type of the Bible

An exposition of Joseph as a type of the written Word, the Bible.
First preached in Martyrs Memorial Church. The text is Genesis 49:22
"Joseph is a fruitful bough, even a fruitful bough by a well; whose branches
run over the wall."

IT HAS BEEN SAID that the New Testament is enfolded in the Old Testament and that the Old Testament is unfolded in the New Testament. The Bible exclaims and proclaims not only the Divine revelation of the God Who wrote it, but also its own nature and divine character. So often when we handle the Scripture and examine its teaching types, its reasoned representations, its marvellous metaphors, its sublime similes and its wonderful symbols, its peculiar personalities and its pure parables we are thinking of these as types of our wonderful Lord, and rightly so.

But in the Old Testament scriptures, these symbols and metaphors and parables and similes also bring out precious truths concerning the divine character and majesty of the Word of God **written**. Of course, we are all aware of Joseph Hart's great lines - "The Scriptures and the Lord bear one tremendous Name; The Written and the Incarnate Word in all things are the same." But I feel we miss some of the glorious unveilings of God's precious written revelation as it is held forth for us in the typology of the Old Testament scriptures.

In the book of Genesis, after Adam, seven representative men step out on to the Scripture page. At their centre stands Abraham, the father of the faithful. When we go back from Abraham, we come to Noah, then to Enoch, then to Abel.

When we go from Abraham, we come to Isaac, and to Jacob. Then to the last of the representative men in Genesis - the wonderful person of the beloved son Joseph. Joseph is one of those characters of the Bible whose sins, defects and imperfections are not recorded. Not that Joseph had no sins, imperfections or defects, but the Holy Spirit chose to major upon those matters concerning Joseph that could be dwelt on in a typical fashion. And what a character Joseph is! There is no doubt that he is a beautiful type of our wonderful Lord. We can see in him, in his journey from the father's house, in the shedding of the coat of many colours, in his affliction and bondage when the iron went into his soul in Egypt, in his provision of bread for the hungry, in his exaltation and marriage to a Gentile bride, facets of the wonderful life and ministry of the only Redeemer of God's elect, the Lord Jesus Christ, our Prophet, Priest and King.

But I want to take Joseph in another sense. I want to speak about Joseph as a type of the **written** Word, the Bible. Turn to Genesis 49 and see the blessings of Jacob upon Joseph. Look at verse 22. "Joseph is a fruitful bough, even a fruitful bough by a well; whose branches run over the wall." There you have the BIOGRA-PHY or the life-story of the Bible.

Then look at the next two verses. "The archers have sorely grieved him, and shot at him, and hated him; but his bow abode in strength, and the arms of his hands were made strong by the hands of the mighty God of Jacob." In those verses you have the BATTLES of the Bible. The Bible is a controversial Book. It is a militant book. It is a book of war - the wars of the Lord. And God is a Man of war.

Then there is a beautiful little parenthesis. Always look at the parentheses of scripture. This parenthesis says "From thence is the Shepherd, the Stone of Israel." I call that the BIBLE of the Bible. We are in the Holiest of all, and there is the Shepherd, the Stone of Israel. The great thing about the book is that if you touch it anywhere, you will touch Christ somewhere. So let us remember the Holiest of all, from whence is the Shepherd, the Stone of Israel.

Then in verse 25, we are launched into a repetition of five blessings. They come from "the God of thy father, Who shall help thee; and by the Almighty (*the El Shaddai, the God All-Sufficient*), Who shall bless thee with blessings of heaven above, blessings of the deep that lieth under, blessings of the breast, and of the womb; the blessings of thy father have prevailed above the blessings of my pro-genitors unto the utmost bound of the everlasting hills." The five-fold BLESS-INGS of the Bible, and thank God this book is a book of blessings - a book of beatitudes, a book of gracious benedictions. Five in scripture is the number of grace, and everything we get from the Bible is by the goodwill of Him that dwelt in the bush. The grace, the mighty, sovereign, unlimited, unchallengable, unalterable grace of Almighty God. "Saved by grace alone; this is all my plea." Thank God for His grace.

Last of all you have a passage concerning "the head of Joseph, and on the crown of the head of him that was separate from his brethren." That is the way the blessing of Moses ends as well. Here we have the BROW of the Bible. It is circled with the glory. "A glory guilds the sacred page, majestic like the sun; It gives a light in every age; it gives and borrows none. The hand that gave it still supplies the gracious light and heat. Its truths upon the nations rise; they rise but never set." Oh, to see the chaplet of the diadem that God has placed upon the Word written. If you turn to Psalm 138:2, you will find there one of the most amazing statements in the whole Bible. "Thou hast magnified Thy Word above all Thy Name." Above the Name, the secret Name, the wonderful Name, the Name that can only be divinely revealed (flesh and blood cannot reveal it unto men), God has put His Word. Oh that we might see the diadem on the brow of the book.

I. THE BIOGRAPHY OF THE BIBLE

Here in a nutshell you have the whole life story of God's Word. "Joseph is a fruitful bough, even a fruitful bough by a well; whose branches run over the wall." Five things lie on the surface of that concerning this book, taking Joseph as a type of the Word. First of all, you have the **designation**. It is a bough. It is a thing of life. It is a plant of renown. It is a plant of God's own planting. That is why the Bible will be with us when heaven and earth have passed away. I have absolute confidence in this Book. It will stand. When the storms are raging and the floods are swelling and the voices of opposition are heard echoing and re-echoing in the corridors of so-called scholarship and ecclesiastical debate I have no fear for God's Word, for it is the plant of God's planting. It is a bough. It has life. Its source and strength is not in itself. Its source and strength is in the God Who planted it. Did you ever notice that God did planting in His creation? There are some interesting matters concerning the planting of God in the first chapters of the book of Genesis. You will notice in Genesis 2:4-5 "These are the generations (*You will be familiar with this expression in the book of Genesis, and which divides up the book*) of the heavens and of the earth when they were created, in the day that the Lord God made the earth and the heavens, and every plant of the field before it was in the earth." Think about that. Some people think that the Lord made the heavens and the earth and plants just started to grow. But they did not. The Lord made them (says the book) before they were in the earth. This old book was made before it was planted in the earth. Man did not utter these words of himself. Man was told to utter them. This is the bough of God's planting.

Notice that every time it is mentioned it is characterised by fruitfulness. Go back to Genesis 49 and look at it carefully. It says "Joseph is a fruitful bough, even a fruitful bough by a well." There you have the **propagation** of the bough. It is fruitful. Literally reading, it is "the son of fertility" - the fertile bough bearing fruit. Nothing could stop Joseph bearing fruit. Nothing can stop the Bible bearing fruit. It must bear fruit, and it will bear fruit. Alas, today, the church has lost its confidence in the power of the Word. This book is fruitful. It bears fruit. They put Joseph into prison, but he still bore fruit. They put his feet into the iron in the prison but he still bore fruit. You could not stop Joseph because although "ye meant it for evil (he said to his brethren) "God meant it for good." Think of the history of the Bible. How many times has the Bible been stripped of its royal robe by the hands of men? How many times has the Bible been put in prison? How many times has it been a banned book discredited and attacked by its enemies, but the wonderful thing about it is this, the book is always fruitful. Nothing can stop the propagation of this book. It is the unstoppable book. They have tried to stop it by fire, by sword, by all the arts and devices of Satan. Take up your Bible. It has been in the fire. There is not a smell of fire upon it. It has been down in the grave. I do not smell death on this book. It is a living book. Those who have abused it and misused it, their names are forgotten, but the old book still lives, and it shall abide for evermore. You see things which are not abiding. Even the heaven above you, and the earth around you, are not abiding, for "heaven and earth shall pass away, but My words shall not pass away." You have something in your hand that will abide for ever - the everlasting book of God. Get this into your hearts and minds. The propagation of this book cannot be stopped.

Look next at the **location**. Where is it? It is "by a well," and it is a well of running water, by a stream. It is by living water. This reminds me of the blessed, ever-freshness of this book. The sustaining of this book is that river clear as crystal that flows from before the throne of God and of the Lamb. The heartbeat of the Bible is the heartbeat of the Son of the Living God, Who lives and abides for ever. You say "Preacher, but I come to this book at times and it seems to me to have no voice." You are not hearing. Sin keeps me from this book. Bless God, this book will keep me from sin. Go back to Psalm 1. "A tree planted by the rivers of water." Oh how fresh is this book! I have come to this book in times of deepest sorrow. I have bemoaned my spiritual estate, brought about by perplexing and conflicting circumstances, but I never came to this book that there was not about it a freshness refreshing the soul in its hour of need. What a book is this! Never forget its location. It is by the water of life. Fresh and fruitful.

Then notice something else. It runs. You read further down about hands and arms. What a sermon could be preached upon the hands and arms of this book. But what about this book running? There you have the **acceleration** of the Word. Paul talks about the Word of God running and having free course and being glorified. What a runner is the book of God! Many of us in our ungodly days tried to run away from God's Word but we could not do it. The Word of God outstripped us and ran after us so fast, and got its arms of arrest around us that we were stopped in our sinful tracks by the power of this Word. May we see again in our day manifestations of the acceleration of God's Word. Have we lost confidence in this book? Is that why the churches are adopting the methods of men, and seeking, having begun in the Spirit to make themselves perfect by the flesh? Is that why the gimmicks are being brought into the church and the things that are fleshly and attractive to the flesh become majors in the church today? I am afraid so. Because people have lost faith in the book. I believe that there is acceleration in the book. It runs. It is a running book. I have just finished some evangelistic meetings in my home town of Ballymena. One of the worst drunkards in the town came to those meetings. His name was a byword. He was a man bound by alcoholism and liquor consumption. One day as the Word was preached it fastened in his heart. He tried to get away from it. He ran hard but he could not outrun the Word. He tried every hidey-hole that the devil could make for him to escape that Word, but the arrows are sharp in the heart of the king's enemy. Overcome by grace divine, he came to Christ, and it is the talk of the town - what God has done for that man's soul. That is the grace of God in the acceleration of the Word. God can do that in one person. He can do it in ten thousand persons. Let us recover our faith in the Word.

Notice finally in this short biography of the Bible, you have the **exaltation** of the Word. This exaltation brings the bough right over the wall. "Whose branches run over the wall." Leaping over walls. That is the history of this Bible. It has leapt over the walls of ages. Read its history. And the Bible that was applicable centuries ago is just as applicable now to this age. It has leapt over the ages and millenniums of time. It leapt over the language barrier. When I take up the Authorised Version of the scriptures it comes home to me in my mother tongue as if it was not a translation but was actually written for me. Because the Bible is the most translatable of all books for it is God's book. Did you ever think of how the Bible leapt over the monastery wall into the heart of Martin Luther? The Pope could not build a wall high enough to keep the Word of God out. Is that not a wonderful thought? At the same preaching series in Ballymena, one night a member of the Royal Ulster Constabulary, a Roman Catholic, was smitten by the Word. He came under the arrest of the Word - could not get away from it, and that evening, as the night shadows gathered, it found him praying the publican's prayer "God be merciful to me the sinner." I think of William Tyndale. How the Bible leapt over the walls of Romanism into that man's soul, soundly converting him, and he took up his pen and fulfilled what he said to that antagonist of his, that "the ploughboy of England would know more of God's Word that thou doest" for he would have it in his mother tongue. Oh let me tell you the Bible leaps over the wall.

II. THE BATTLES OF THE BIBLE

"The archers have sorely grieved him, and shot at him, and hated him, but his bow abode in strength, and the arms of his hands were made strong by the hands of the Mighty God of Jacob." In ancient times weapons were different from today. For long distance conflict the weapon was the arrow. For short distance combat the weapon was the sword or the spear. Here we have the archers, or the masters of arrows. We know who they were in the life of Joseph. They were the members of his own household. How they shot at Joseph, leading to his sale into Egypt, his accusation and imprisonment in the land of Pharaoh. The masters of the arrows did their work. You can look at the history of the battles of the Bible and they are all set forth here as in a nutshell. Notice three things that are highlighted here. THE STRATEGY OF THE BIBLE'S FOOLS. They do three things. They are out to grieve Joseph. They are out to shoot at Joseph. They are out to hate Joseph.

Now this Bible of mine has been subjected to a series of perversions that **grieve** the blessed Word of God. I am referring to modern translations of our English language. I make no apology for saying that when a Bible refuses to allow in its pages worship to the Son of God - as the New English Bible does - that is a perversion of Holy Scripture. The NEB will give worship to the devil and to idols but not to the Son of God. There are a whole series of mutilated translations of God's Holy and Blessed book around today. When you walk into a Bible shop and say "I want a copy of the Bible," they say to you "Which Bible would you like?" as if God wrote about 50 Bibles, and you make your choice. Thank you very much, I will be sticking to the old Authorised Version. The old is the best, because this translation has upon it the signal blessings of the Blessed Holy Ghost coming to us directly from the great Protestant Pentecost. What is more, it is the Bible from which the Puritans and the great men of the church preached and in which they believed. They can call me old-fashioned, or any other name they like, but I will be sticking to this old book. My soul is grieved when I see God's people carrying to God's house perverted versions of God's Word. Ask the new Bible Who God is. You get the answer. Ask Who Jesus Christ is. He is the son of a young woman, not the son of the virgin. Talk about being grieved - this Bible has been grieved.

But there is something more. It has been **shot at**. It has become the target. Joseph was the target of enemies in his own house. And in the professing church, the Bible has been targeted for vicious, diabolical attacks by so-called clergymen, and even Bishops of the Established Church. May we have our eyes open to see the attack that has been made upon this blessed book. Do you know why it is attacked? It is attacked because it is **hated**. And do you know why it is hated? It is hated because people do not like the truth that it speaks. Why are God's servants hated? They are hated because they say things that people do not like. This Bible says things that people do not like. I had an interview with Mr Callaghan, former Prime Minister. He said to me, "Ian, we are all children of God." I said, "Is that right?" "Oh yes," he said "we are all children of God." I said "With due respect to you and your office, Sir, I prefer to believe the Lord Jesus Christ rather than you. And Jesus Christ did not say that we are all children of God. In fact, He referred to certain religious people as children of the devil." When I said that he nearly fell off his seat. And then he said, "We are not going to discuss the Scriptures." I said "I did not raise the matter, but if you raise any matter relevant to the scriptures, I will be answering you." I had word from one of his relations who said in her letter "You were getting too near the quick," because Mr Callaghan made a profession of faith and was baptised by immersion and was received into the Baptist Church. That is why he responded like that. The Word was going home. People do not like the book because the book tells them the truth. If a man preaches the book he will not be liked. You show me a man who has no enemies, and I will show you a man that does not preach the book. You show me a man that has plenty of enemies, and I will show you a man that is standing preaching God's unvarnished truth without fear or favour. There will always be opposition to the Bible. Remember the threefold strategy - they grieve him, they shoot at him, and they hate him.

Then notice secondly, that there is here THE SECRET OF THE BIBLE'S FORCE. Why is the Bible such a powerful book? The Bible has a great hand upon it. "The arms of his hands were made strong by the hands of the Mighty God of Jacob." Do you remember the story of the death of Elisha? The king came to see him. And he said to the king "Put an arrow in the bow and stand at the window." And that old weak prophet put a trembling hand over the hand of the young king; and another hand over his other hand. He helped the king to fire the arrow of the Lord's deliverance. The weak hand of Elisha upon the strong hand of the king. But here we have it reversed, we have the weak hand of the man overshadowed by the strong hand of God. That is the secret of the Bible's strength. Behind the Bible is the hand of the Almighty. If you look at the life of Jacob, you will see how many times the strong hand of God delivered Jacob. May we crave for the covering of the Lord's hand! I was thinking of another portion of Scripture. "I give unto My sheep eternal life; and they shall never perish, neither shall any man pluck them out of My hand; My Father, which gave them Me, is greater than all; and no man is able to pluck them out of My Father's hand." Praise God, we have the hand of Jesus and the covering hand of the Father. That is the strength of this book. This book has its power in God. God, Who with a word spoke the heavens into existence and called the earth from the bosom of nothingness into existence, has graciously given that word and set it, embalmed it in this book. What a word it is - the word of the Living God. That is the secret of the Bible's force.

But lastly notice THE STEADFASTNESS OF THE BIBLE'S FIGHT. "His bow abode in strength." It still remains strong. The bows of the wicked are broken but the bow of God still remains in its strength. There is a word in Psalm 64:3-9 "Who whet their tongue like a sword, and bend their bow to shoot their arrows, even bitter words; that they may shoot in secret at the perfect; suddenly do they shoot at him, and fear not. They encourage themselves in an evil matter: they commune of laying snares privily; they say, Who shall see them? They search out iniquities; they accomplish a diligent search; but the inward thought of every one of them, and the heart, is deep. But God shall shoot at them" Hallelujah! "with an arrow; suddenly shall they be wounded. So they shall make their own tongue to fall upon themselves; all that see them shall flee away. And all men shall fear, and shall declare the work of God; for they shall wisely consider of His doing." His bow abode in strength. May God teach us how to fire the arrows. Jeremiah said "Spare no arrows against Babylon." How we need preachers that will spare no gospel arrows against the apostasy of this our day and generation. But in that portion about the battles of the Bible there is the parenthesis "From thence is the Shepherd, the Stone of Israel." I call it

III. THE BIBLE OF THE BIBLE

We have come to the Holiest of all. It is interesting to note that there are four "froms" here. "But his bow abode in strength for the arms of his hands were made strong by" the word is *"from"* "the hands of the Mighty God of Jacob." And *"from* thence is the Shepherd." Then "even by" or *from* "the God of thy father Who shall help thee; and by" or *from* "the Almighty." Where does the Shepherd come from? He comes from God, for He Himself is God. How wonderful that the first of these titles of Christ describes the work of THE SHEPHERD. Jacob was a shepherd. For twenty years in winter storms and summer heat he shepherded the flock of Laban his father-in-law. He knew the drought of the summer and the icy chills of the winter. He was a shepherd. But his eye was toward another Shepherd, the Shepherd of the flock of God, described in the New Testament in three ways - as the Good Shepherd, the Great Shepherd, and the Chief Shepherd.

The **Good Shepherd** brings me to the cross. "I am the Good Shepherd; the Good Shepherd giveth His life for the sheep." That is a lovely text. It was on that text that I came to know the Saviour many years ago, after listening to a children's address given by my beloved mother, who is now herself in the glory land. So when I read that verse, I say "That is Ian Paisley's text." That is the rock that carried me to the cross.

But we come a little further. "Who brought again from the dead that **Great Shepherd** of the sheep." We have come to the empty tomb. He was delivered because of our offences. He is raised again to justify us? No, sir. He is raised again because we are justified. If the mighty sin debt for His people had not been fully cancelled, the devil would still hold the mortgage on the body of Christ. "Who is he that condemneth? It is Christ that died, yea, rather that is risen again." The body of Christ could not lie in that tomb because the debt is fully paid. He gave

His life as the Good Shepherd. He arose as the Great Shepherd. What to do? To bring many sons into glory. And He is bringing them. He is shepherding them along the way. You know, He shepherded us, even when we were running to hell. He preserved me when my feet made haste to hell. And there I would have been but God did all things well. His love was great, His grace was free that from hell's pit delivered me. That old missionary from the Church of Scotland to the Jewish nation rose one morning and said to his Scottish congregation that he was going to preach upon a great text in Isaiah 53. "He shall see His seed." And he took a great outline. He said: 1, He shall see His seed born and brought in; 2, He shall see His seed educated and brought up; 3, He shall see His seed supported and brought through; 4, He shall see His seed glorified and brought home. Who is He? He is the Great Shepherd. But that is not the end of the story. I have been at the cross, I have seen the empty tomb.

But thank God, there is the open heaven. The **Chief Shepherd** is going to appear. Jesus Christ is coming again, visibly, gloriously, majestically, victoriously. He is coming. The church today has forgotten the message of this Coming Lord. The heavens and the earth will one day shake when the great last trumpet sounds and the dead in Christ shall rise and be changed, and we that are alive and remain shall be caught up together with them in the clouds, to meet the Lord in the air. So shall we ever be with the Lord. The Chief Shepherd will bring in every lamb of the flock and every sheep of the pasture of God.

But He is not only the Shepherd. He is THE STONE. The Stone speaks to me of the Stone that the builders rejected. He has become the Headstone of the corner. "Our Lord is now rejected and by the world disowned, by the many still neglected and by the few enthroned; But soon He'll come in glory, the hour is drawing nigh, in the crowning day that's coming by and by. That stone cut out without hands shall fill the whole earth. Then shall the kingdoms of this world become the kingdoms of our Lord and of His Christ and He shall reign - glorious prospect of the church of Jesus Christ. That is our blessed hope. Do you revel in it? Do you rejoice in it? Do you purify yourself daily because of it?

IV. THE BLESSINGS OF THE BIBLE

They are very suggestive. "The blessing of the **heaven above**, blessings of the **deep that lieth under**." You know the first time the heavens were opened and the deep that lieth under was opened, was at the time of Noah's flood. They were opened in destruction on sinners but they were opened in deliverance for God's chosen people. The floods that destroyed the world lifted Noah's ark and helped him to outsail the storm until he landed in a newly-washed earth. There is a blessing which comes from above to the children of God. It is in this book. There is a blessing of the deep that comes to the people of God through this book.

Then there is the blessing of child-bearing, of a nursing church. I am afraid that the church today is not a nursing church. How seldom do we hear the cry of newborn babes in God's house? How seldom do we hear the cry of newborn children longing for the sincere milk of the Word that they may grow thereby? How long is it since we have seen the evident manifestation of God bringing children through unto the birth at the preaching of His Word? The nursing fathers and the nursing mothers in the church are scarce today. When Zion travaileth, she bringeth forth. But the travails of Zion are not known today. Men and women of God do not groan and pray and sigh for the birth of souls. But thank God, this book brings the blessing of the **birth** and of the **breasts**.

It does something else. It brings "the blessings of **the father**." We often talk about our father's God. Thank God some of us have had godly parents. The greatest blessing next to being a child of God is to be a child of God's children. I thank God that I was given that blessing. I was born into a Christian home - into the home of a man of God, who loved the book and instilled into my heart reverence for this precious Word. Our father's God still lives and the blessing that came to our fathers came only through the channel of God's Word. "An evil and adulterous generation seeketh after a sign, but no sign shall be given to it but the sign of Jonah." What was that sign? It was the sign of the resurrection of our blessed Lord. And I tell you that this book is the only channel through which God's blessing flows. It is back to the Bible that we need to come, back to this old book, with reverent hearts and contrite spirits and in submission to God's will.

Then you will notice that Jacob says "my blessings have exceeded the blessings of my **progenitors** unto the utmost bound of the everlasting hills." There is no limit to the blessings of God Almighty. You cannot limit those blessings.

Turn to Deuteronomy 33:13-16 and you will notice that these blessings run parallel with precious things. There are precious things in this book. Thank God for eyes to see the precious things that are in the Word of God. There are "precious things of heaven, for the dew, and for the deep that coucheth beneath ... precious fruits brought forth by the sun " precious things put forth by the moon." There are precious things of the light and there are precious things of the night. Do not miss the night scenes of Scripture. For every child of God has to walk through the night-times. But you know what the Lord does. He giveth me songs in the night. Do you know anything about night-singing, as a child of God? And "precious things of the lasting hills and ... precious things of the earth, and fullness thereof, and for the goodwill of Him that dwelt in the bush." They are all gifts of grace. Start looking for the precious things in this book.

V. THE BROW OF THE BIBLE

"They shall be on the head of Joseph, and on the crown of the head of him that was separated from his brethren." God has crowned this book with a diadem. He has crowned it with a chaplet of victory and a crown of the purest gold, magnified it above His wonderful Name. We should approach the book with submission because it is God-centred. It calls for and demands instantaneous obedience from His children. We should approach the book with joy. Every lasting joy the child of God has, comes through confidence begotten in the heart by this Word. This book is the creator of faith. "Faith cometh by hearing, and hearing by the Word of God." Do not come to me and say "Preacher, how can I have more faith? Read the book. That is the way you get faith. Soak yourself in the book. Bathe in the book. "Now ye are clean through the Word that I have spoken unto you ... If ye abide in Me, and My words abide in you." What joy we miss because we do not see the circle of gold on the brow of the book. This is God's book, God's precious book, given to us that we might have a touch of heaven upon earth; a compass to direct our barque through the reefs and through all the storms of life's sea. What a book it is! I have a few words written in the front of my Bible. "When thou goest, it shall lead thee; when thou sleepest, it shall keep thee; and when thou awakest it shall talk with thee; for the commandment is a lamp; and the law is light: and the reproofs of instruction are the way of life" (Proverbs 6:22-33). Does it lead you? When you sleep, does its keep you? When you are awake, does it talk to you? Is it a lamp to your soul? Is it a light to your way? Is it reproofs of instruction? Oh that God would help us to obey Isaiah 34:16 "Seek ye out of the book of the Lord, and read. Also Deuteronomy 11:18 "Therefore shall ye lay up these words in your heart, and in your soul." May we love this book because it leads us to the Lover of our souls, even He Who is all the glory in Immanuel's land.

5 The Ten
Commandments

AN EXPOSITION OF THE TEN COMMANDMENTS IN TWO SERMONS PREACHED IN THE
MARTYRS MEMORIAL CHURCH IN AUGUST 1993.

AT THE REFORMATION THE Reformers ordered off the communion table
the reserved sacrament or, as it was called, the transubstantiated wafer.

The only time the elements of bread and wine were permitted on the
table was at the service of the Lord's Supper.

At other times the open Bible was displayed upon the table - the Word of
God. Many years ago, after visiting Calvin's cathedral in Geneva, I decided to follow that practice in this house.

Another practice the Reformers instigated was that the ten commandments
should be displayed in a paramount place so that God's moral law should be kept
before the people.

I have remedied my oversight in this matter and had my daughter Rhonda
letter the ten commandments and these will be displayed in the porch of the
church. This work has been tastefully executed. They are worth several hundreds
of pounds and are a gift to the church.

THE GREAT UNDERLYING PRINCIPLE OF THE ECONOMIES

In my sermon today I want to speak upon the two tables of the law. You
will remember that the commandments were originally written by the finger of
God on two tables of stone.

This two-fold division of the commandments I will come to as I proceed with my sermon.

When Satan challenged Christ's Godhead in the first temptation the answer which our Lord gave him was most authoritative, most emphatic and most compelling: *"Man shall not live by bread alone but by every word of God."* - Luke 4: 4.

Now note carefully, this great principle underlies each economy of God which man, God's creation, has lived under.

When man was in Eden's garden in the beauty of his created holiness, unfallen and unspotted by sin, the command to him in order to maintain and live in that sinless state was enunciated to him by God Himself.

"And the Lord God commanded the man, saying, Of every tree of the garden thou mayest freely eat: But of the tree of the knowledge of good and evil, thou shalt not eat of it: for in the day that thou eatest thereof thou shalt surely die." - Genesis 2: 16-17

So in the original economy under which man first lived, this principle was its greatest foundation. Man cannot live by bread alone but by every word of God.

After the fall and the bringing in of the Mosaic economy the same principle was enunciated once more as its foundation.

"And he humbled thee, and suffered thee to hunger, and fed thee with manna, which thou knewest not, neither did thy fathers know; that he might make thee know that man doth not live by bread alone, but by every word that proceedeth out of the mouth of the Lord doth man live." - Deuteronomy 8: 3.

Following the Mosaic economy there came the Prophetic economy. In it yet again the principle was enunciated.

"So shall my word be that goeth forth out of my mouth ... it shall not return unto me void but it shall accomplish that which I please." - Isaiah 55: 11.

Then when the Christian economy was ushered in by our Lord Himself the basic principle was once more promulgated.

"But he answered and said, It is written, Man shall not live by bread alone, but by every word that proceedeth out of the mouth of God." Matthew 4: 4

"And Jesus answered him, saying, It is written, That man shall not live by bread alone, but by every word of God." - Luke 4:4

When Paradise is regained the heavenly economy will rest upon the same impregnable foundation.

"Thy kingdom come. Thy will be done in earth, as it is in heaven." - Matthew 6: 10.

God's will is found in His Word.

"Blessed are they that do his commandments, that they may have right to the tree of life, and may enter in through the gates into the city." - Revelation 22: 14.

So the common, underlying foundation of the Paradisical, Mosaic, Prophetic, Christian and Heavenly economies lays the axe to the root of hyperdispensationalism so prominent in many so-called Fundamentalist churches to day. The Bible is one, its Gospel is one, its Church is one.

There are two verses in the Bible which are worthy of careful comparison and contrast when we are considering this very important theme.

The first text is in the Old Testament. It is the word of the royal preacher Solomon.

"Let us hear the conclusion of the whole matter: Fear God, and keep his commandments: for this is the whole duty of man." - Ecclesiastes 12: 13.

Note "duty" is in italics in the Authorised Version. In the original it reads "the whole man". Mark the word "whole". He is not a whole man, a healed man, a complete man, except he lives by every word which proceedeth out of the mouth of God.

The second text is in the New Testament in James 2: 10

"For whosoever shall keep the whole law, and yet offend in one point, he is guilty of all."

Note the common denominator in both texts is the word "whole". The whole man - the whole law.

The law is one. It is whole. To violate one commandment is to violate them all. Keeping nine is not enough.

The ten commandments are the ten sides of the one perfect, sublime, revealed law of God.

It is by every word which proceeded out of God's mouth that we alone can live. Violate one word and you die.

Moses in his great farewell song to Israel had this to say about the giving of the law and its character.

"And he said, The Lord came from Sinai, and rose up from Seir unto them; he shined forth from mount Paran, and he came with ten thousands of saints: from his right hand went a fiery law for them. Yea, he loved the people;

all his saints are in thy hand: and they sat down at thy feet; every one shall receive of thy words." - Deuteronomy 33: 2-3.

Note the words "Yes, he loved the people". The severity of the Triune God's thrice-holy law is the only possible outcome of his thrice-holy love. His eternal heart has this one ultimate purpose, to bring again to perfection fallen man, and to a perfection which never again can be violated or destroyed.

You and I can never know the perfection of God's love until we behold the perfection of God's law nor can we know the perfection of God's law until we behold the perfection of God's love.

There is a word in the first chapter of John's Gospel we need to remember always.

"For the law was given by Moses, but grace and truth came by Jesus Christ." - John 1: 17.

Notice the order of Christ's operation "grace and truth". We cannot know the truth of God first. It's blinding holiness would devour and destroy us unless we have first partaken of God's grace. Remember also what Christ called the weightier matters of the law, judgment, mercy and faith (Matthew 23: 23). These characterise the pure gospel of Sovereign Grace.

THE DIVISIONS OF THE TEN COMMANDMENTS

It is crystal clear that the commandments commence in Exodus 20: 2. Verse one tells us "And *God spake all these words saying."* Then commence God's words verse 2. It is highly important that this is noted. What is more, the words, *"The Lord Thy God"* occur in the first five commandments. In the first commandment in verse 2, in the second commandment in verse 5, in the third commandment in verse 7, in the fourth commandment in verse 10, and in the fifth commandment in verse 12. These words put a special mark on the first five commandments and constitute their distinct difference from the other five. Their emphasis is upon our relationship towards God.

The other five emphasise our relationship towards our neighbours. We know that God wrote them on two tables of stone (Exodus 31: 18) and Christ confirmed for us that their division was not four and six but five and five, in Matthew 22 verses 37-40: *"Jesus said unto him, Thou shalt love the Lord thy God with all thy heart, and with all thy soul, and with all thy mind. This is the first and great commandment. And the second is like unto it, Thou shalt love thy neigh-*

bour as thyself. On these two commandments hang all the law and the proph-ets." The first is in relation to loving. Note the operative word the *Lord thy God,* verse 37 and the second in relationship to loving thy neighbour in verse 39. Note, not thy parents but thy neighbour, for commandment five is in the first division written on the first table of the law.

The Roman Catholic church does away with the second commandment. Its teaching strikes so hard at her graven images before which she teaches her people to bow down and serve. In order to find a tenth to take the place of the second, Rome divides God's tenth commandment into two parts. "Thou shalt not covet thy neighbour's wife" is Rome's ninth. "Thou shalt not covet thy neighbour's goods" is Rome's tenth. This is an unscriptural division and impossible without rending the text.

The structures of the tenth commandment are:-

1. **General** Thy neighbour's house.
2. **Particular** (a) wife, servant, maid (human).
   (b) ox and ass (animal).
3. **General** Anything that is thy neighbour's.

What God has joined together let no man put asunder. The Roman Antichrist is a rich specialist in this great sin of rending asunder what God has united.

CHRIST'S SEAL TO THE TEN COMMANDMENTS

Christ put His seal upon each of the ten commandments.

The First, Matthew 22: 37: *"Jesus said unto him, Thou shalt love the Lord thy God with all thy heart, and with all thy soul, and with all thy mind."*

The Second, John 4: 24: *"God is a Spirit: and they that worship him must worship him in spirit and in truth."*

The Third, Matthew 5: 34: *"But I say unto you, Swear not at all; neither by heaven; for it is God's throne."*

The Fourth, Mark 2: 27: *"And he said unto them, The sabbath was made for man, and not man for the sabbath."* Luke 13: 14-16: *"And the ruler of the synagogue answered with indignation, because that Jesus had healed on the sabbath day, and said unto the people. There are six days in which men ought to work: in them therefore come and be healed, and not on the sabbath day. The Lord then answered him, and said, Thou hypocrite, doth not each one of you on the sabbath loose his ox or his ass from the stall, and lead him away to watering?"*

The Fifth, Matthew 15: 4-6: *"For God commanded, saying Honour thy father and mother: and, He that curseth father or mother, let him die the death. But ye say, Whosoever shall say to his father or his mother, It is a gift, by whatsoever thou mightest be profited by me. And honour not his father or his mother, he shall be free. Thus have ye made the commandment of God of none effect by your tradition."* Matthew 19: 19: *"Honour thy father and thy mother: and, Thou shalt love thy neighbour as thyself."* Mark 7: 10: *"For Moses said, Honour thy father and thy mother; and, Whoso curseth father or mother, let him die the death."*

The Sixth, Matthew 5: 21: *"Ye have heard that it was said by them of old time, Thou shalt not kill; and whosoever shall kill shall be in danger of the judgment."*

The Seventh: Matthew 5: 28: *"But I say unto you, That whosoever looketh on a woman to lust after her hath committed adultery with her already in his heart."* Matthew 19: 9: *"And I say unto you, Whosoever shall put away his wife, except it be for fornication, and shall marry another committeth adultery: and whoso marrieth her which is put away doth commit adultery. "* Matthew 19: 18: *"He that saith unto him, Which? Jesus said, Thou shalt do no murder, Thou shalt not commit adultery, Thou shalt not steal,. Thou shalt not bear false witness."*

The Eighth, Matthew 15: 19: *" For out of the heart proceed evil thoughts, murders, adulteries, fornications, thefts, false witness, blasphemies."*

The Ninth, Matthew 12: 34-37: *O generation of vipers, how can ye, being evil, speak good things? for out of the abundance of the heart the mouth speaketh. A good man out of the good treasure of the heart bringeth forth good things: and an evil man out of the evil treasure bringeth forth evil things. But I say unto you. That every idle word that men shall speak, they shall give account thereof in the day of judgment. For by thy words thou shalt be justified, and by thy words thou shalt be condemned."*

The Tenth, Matthew 5: 28: *"But I say unto you, That whosoever looketh on a woman to lust after her hath committed adultery with her already in his heart."*

Each Commandment has been confirmed by Christ.

THE FIRST FIVE COMMANDMENTS

The first five commandments relate to PIETY, our worship of God.

The second five commandments relate to PROBITY, uprightness and honesty to man.

We are now going to look at the first five.

These five begin with the first, calling for honour to God and end with the fifth calling for honour to our parents, whom God has specially honoured. By honouring our parents we honour God. This has nothing to do with neighbour relationship. Relationships with our neighbour fall under the second five commandments, commandments six to ten.

THE THEME

The theme of the first five commandments is the true worship of the true God. The first commandment's theme is the purity of worship. The second commandment's theme is the prohibitions of true worship. The third commandment's theme is the penalty for violating true worship. The fourth commandment's theme is the provision of true worship. The fifth commandment's theme is the promise of true worship.

DIVINE SUMMARY

The words of Christ to the Samaritan woman are a Divine summary of the first five commandments and the best possible comment upon them.

"But the hour cometh, and now is, when the true worshippers shall worship the Father in spirit and in truth: for the Father seeketh such to worship him. God is a Spirit: and they that worship him must worship him in spirit and in truth." - John 4: 23-24.

They indicate the principles and practices of the true worship of the only true God.

I. THE PURITY OF TRUE WORSHIP

The only true God alone is the object of true worship. No rival can be tolerated. The temple is the temple of God alone and can never ever be a pantheon, a temple of many gods. Now it must be understood at the outset that no man can keep God's law as the way to life and thus merit salvation.

"Therefore by the deeds of the law there shall no flesh be justified in his sight: for by the law is the knowledge of sin." - Romans 3: 20.

Life cannot be obtained by keeping the law and none can keep it for there is none righteous, no, not one.

"As it is written, There is none righteous, no, not one." - Romans 3: 10.

But the law is the way of life after we have been redeemed and justified freely by His grace. (Being not without law to God but under law to Christ. 1 Corinthians 9: 21).

Therefore the first words of this commandment are of vital importance.

"I am the Lord thy God, which have brought thee out of the land of Egypt, out of the house of bondage." - Exodus 20: 2.

There are three great truths which are here revealed.

1. Relationship - "I am the Lord thy God".
2. Redemption - "which brought thee out of the land of Egypt".
3. Release - "out of the house of bondage".

It is only as we enjoy by free grace alone the benefits of God's relationship, God's redemption and God's release that we can joyfully keep the ten commandments as our way of living.

1. RELATIONSHIP

The initiative comes from God. He originated His work in our hearts. We are not saved by our meritorious works but by His free, unmerited, undeserved favour. *"Herein is love, not that we loved God but that God loved us."* - 1 John 4: 10. He has chosen us as His own - *"I am the Lord thy God."* Why? Just because He loved us.

"For thou art an holy people unto the Lord thy God: the Lord thy God hath chosen thee to be a special people unto himself, above all people that are upon the face of the earth. The Lord did not set his love upon you, nor choose you, because ye were more in number than any people; for ye were the fewest of all people: But because the Lord loved you, and because he would keep the oath which he had sworn unto your fathers, hath the Lord brought you out with a mighty hand, and redeemed you out of the house of bondmen, from the hand of Pharaoh king of Egypt." - Deuteronomy 7: 6-8.

He is the Lord - Jehovah. That title signifies His Self-Sufficiency, Eternality, Sovereignty, Immutability.

"For I am the Lord, I change not; therefore ye sons of Jacob are not consumed." - Malachi 3: 6.

He says, *"I am the Lord thy God"* we respond, *"This God is our God He will be our guide even unto death."* - Psalm 48: 14.

2. REDEMPTION

"Which brought thee out of the land of Egypt."
That redemption was by the blood shedding, the blood sprinkling and the blood sheltering of the blood of the Passover lamb.
Christ, our Passover is sacrificed for us.
"Purge out therefore the old leaven, that ye may be a new lump, as ye are unleavened. For even Christ our Passover is sacrificed for us." - 1 Corinthians 5: 7.
Through His blood of redemption we are covenanted to be the Lord's. We therefore love His law, it is our delight.
"More to be desired are they than gold, yea, than much fine gold: sweeter also than honey and the honeycomb." -Psalm 19: 10.
"Moreover by them is thy servant warned: and in keeping of them there is great reward." - Psalm 19: 11.

3. RELEASE

"And of the house of bondage"
Emancipation resulting from redemption. Liberty the result of salvation. Release from the law as the way to life. Released to be under the law as the way of life.
Relationship, redemption and release. These are the pillars upon which my glad obedience to the Lord my God rests. These motivate me to cling to Him alone and reject, repudiate and refuse all other gods.
Two verses from Romans chapter three sum up the whole position of the person who is enabled to worship God in Spirit and in truth, and offer up pure and acceptable worship to Him:
"But now the righteousness of God without the law is manifested, being witnessed by the law and the prophets; Even the righteousness of God which is by faith of Jesus Christ unto all and upon all them that believe: for there is no difference." - Romans 3: 21-22.

II. THE PROHIBITIONS OF TRUE WORSHIP

"Thou shalt not make unto thee any graven image, or any likeness of any thing that is in heaven above, or that is in the earth beneath, or that is in the

water under the earth: Thou shalt not bow down thyself to them, nor serve them: for I the Lord thy God am a jealous God, visiting the iniquity of the fathers upon the children unto the third and fourth generation of them that hate me; And shewing mercy unto thousands of them that love me, and keep my commandments." - Exodus 20: 3-6.

God has revealed Himself to us, He has also revealed the way we should worship Him. He only is God and to no one else has worship to be given, therefore all religious reverence and worship for anyone else or anything else strikes at the heart of true worship and is a violation of this commandment. This commandment is clear and unmistakably plain. All intrusion and intruders into God's worship are idolatrous impostures and impostors. Anything or anyone which usurps the place of Christ as sole mediator between God and man is here prohibited.

This commandment does not forbid the making of likenesses as for civil or historical uses but forbids the making of likenesses for religious use in forms and acts of worship.

The prohibitions of true worship are that any such likeness for religious purposes should not be made and where made must not be bowed down to or served.

Such an image is a lie. God is spiritual essence and cannot be worshipped by man's hands.

The Roman Antichrist excels in violating this commandment by making images of Christ, the Virgin Mary and multitudes of angels and saints. She further adds to her iniquity by deleting this commandment altogether from her teaching catechism.

Thomas Watson, the great Presbyterian pastor, was right when he said: *"Go not into their chapels to see their crucifixes, or hear mass; as the looking on a harlot draws to adultery, so the looking on the popish gilded picture may draw to idolatry. Take heed the popish priests do not rob you of your principles, and defile you with their images."*

God is a jealous God. His very name is Jealous.

"For thou shalt worship no other god: for the Lord, whose name is Jealous, is a jealous God." - Exodus 34: 14.

He is jealous because of His love for us. He is jealous lest we should go after false gods. God cannot bear a co-rival. His spouse must be faithful. Idolatry causes God to visit His people in punishment. Idolatry in iniquitous in His sight.

It is a contaminating apostasy reaching to the third and fourth generation and indicted by God as hatred of Himself.

He that setteth up an image and bows before and worships it hates God. All idolaters are God haters. Note however the glorious note of gospel grace which also sounds in this commandment. Note the very punishment is not lengthened in vengeance but distributed in mercy over the third and fourth generations so that the whole weight of the punishment falls not on the first and second generation. Oh there is mercy with God even in judgment. In wrath He remembers mercy. Then there is a display of His mercy rich, full, free and abundant:

"Showing mercy upon thousands of them." Where sin abounded grace super-abounds. We can force God to punish us but not to pardon us. His mercy is free.

"That love me." This love is begotten by His love for us. We love Him because he first loved us. 1 John 4: 19.

"And keep His commandments." Love and obedience are divine twins, they walk hand in hand.

"Blessed are they that keep judgment, and he that doeth righteousness at all times." - Psalm 106: 3.

Surely here in this commandment of the prohibitions of true worship, we have exhibition of the weightier matters of the law - judgment, mercy and faith - the gospel itself.

III. THE PENALTY OF VIOLATING TRUE WORSHIP

"Thou shalt not take the name of the Lord thy God in vain; for the Lord will not hold him guiltless-that taketh his name in vain." - Exodus 20: 7.

True worship demands that we *"fear this glorious and fearful name, the Lord thy God"* - Deuteronomy 28: 28.

We take God's name in vain when we speak lightly and irreverently of His name, when we profess His name with our lips but deny it by our lives, when we use it in idle conversation, when we worship Him with our lips but our hearts are far from Him, when we do not believe on His name, when we profane His name in any way, when we listen to such profanity, when we swear by His name, and when we speak against Him.

By doing any of these or in any way making light of God's Holy name there comes a guiltiness and that guiltiness will be called to God's bar of judgment and we will be made answerable for it.

The Lord will not hold him guiltless that taketh His name in vain. You may hold yourself guiltless, society may hold you guiltless, but God will not hold you guiltless. May that solemn threat lock our tongues and bolt our lips from taking God's name in vain.

IV. THE PRIVILEGE OF TRUE WORSHIP

"Remember the sabbath day, to keep it holy. Six days shalt thou labour, and do all thy work: But the seventh day is the sabbath of the Lord thy God: in it thou shalt not do any work, thou nor thy son, nor thy daughter, thy manservant, nor thy maidservant, nor thy cattle, nor thy stranger that is within thy gates: For in six days the Lord made heaven and earth, the sea, and all that in them is, and rested the seventh day: wherefore the Lord blessed the sabbath day, and hallowed it." - Exodus 28: 8-11.

God hath appointed one day in seven for man to enjoy the full privilege of true worship.

The day has been changed but the command to keep the day holy has not been changed.

THE CREATION SABBATH

"And on the seventh day God ended his work which he had made; and he rested on the seventh day from all his work which he had made. And God blessed the seventh day, and sanctified it: because that in it he had rested from all his work which God created and made." - Genesis 2: 2-3.

The basis for keeping the Creation Sabbath was creation itself. *"For in six days the Lord made heaven and earth"*. But the Creation Sabbath was a Prophetic Sabbath. It prophesied of a greater creation, the new creation of Christ and its completion.

THE MOSAIC REDEMPTION SABBATH

"And remember that thou wast a servant in the land of Egypt, and that the Lord thy God brought thee out thence through a mighty hand and by a stretched out arm: therefore the Lord thy God commanded thee to keep the sabbath day." - Deuteronomy 5: 15.

The basis for keeping the Mosaic Sabbath was redemption from Egypt. But the Mosaic Sabbath was also a Prophetic Sabbath. It prophesied of a great redemption, the Sabbath of the Redemption that is in Christ Jesus.

The prophetic fulfilment of the Old Creation Sabbaths were fulfilled at Calvary when the new Creation was completed and the new redemption accomplished.

Christ in glorious fulfilment of the Old Sabbaths made a new day - the Lord's Day, the Christian Sabbath.

"The stone which the builders refused is become the head stone of the corner. This is the Lord's doing; it is marvellous in our eyes. This is the day which the Lord hath made; we will rejoice and be glad in it." - Psalm 118: 22-24.

This day of privilege for true worship should be our delight. We should be glad in it, rejoice in it and use it to praise our God.

We should be diligent in this godless age to show by our conduct on the Lord's Day that we are on the Lord's side. We should prepare for the Lord's Day. We should sacredly observe the Lord's Day. We should sanctify the Lord's Day by reading, listening to, meditating on, imparting to others, and praying over, God's Word.

We should be diligent in our attendance at the House of God and we should order our homes to love the Day of God.

V. THE PROMISE OF TRUE WORSHIP

"Honour thy father and thy mother: that thy days may be long upon the land which the Lord thy God giveth thee." - Exodus 20: 12.

This commandment brings the family in to the sphere of worship and it ends with promise. It is the first commandment with promise. God has honoured parentage. Fathers and mothers have a special place of honour with God. We honour God when we honour those whom He has commanded us to honour. Note the mother's place in the plane of honour in her own sphere in the home.

Fathers in the state, fathers in society, fathers in the church all should be honoured as they honour God. The New Testament comment on this commandment in its civic and social bearing is Romans 13: 1-5:

"Let every soul be subject unto the higher powers. For there is no power but of God: the powers that be are ordained of God. Whosoever therefore resisteth the power, resisteth the ordinance of God: and they that resist shall receive to themselves damnation. For rulers are not a terror to good works, but to the evil. Wilt thou then not be afraid of the power? do that which is good, and thou shalt have praise of the same: For he is the minister of God to thee for good. But if thou do that which is evil, be afraid; for he beareth not the sword in vain: for he is the minister of God, a revenger to execute wrath upon him that doeth evil. Wherefore ye must needs be subject, not only for wrath but also for conscience sake."

Now true worship in conformity to God's Word gives the promise of the life that now is and of the life that is hereafter. Here is the promise: *"That thy days may be long in the land which the Lord thy God giveth thee."* Notice the first gift of God - the land. Notice the second gift of God - the health to enjoy the land. Holiness is health, true worship enables a man to live, for man cannot live but by every word of God.

These five commandments show us the way. Do them and thou shalt live with a life which all hell cannot extinguish and all heaven cannot exhaust. This is life indeed!

IT SHOULD BE REMEMBERED that God's law was given in Arabia, the same country which witnessed the giving of Mohammed's law. Allah's law was the devil's challenge to Jehovah's law and usurped the same country for its promulgation. It continues to this day in its wicked usurpation.

In looking at all ten commandments, their contents can be summarised under three points:-
1. Commandments One and Two are in the sphere of **Thought**.
2. Commandment Three is in the sphere of **Word**.
3. Commandments Four and Five are in the sphere of **Deed**.
   In the second five the order is inversed:-
1. Commandments Six, Seven and Eight are in the sphere of **Deed**.
2. Commandment Nine is in the sphere of **Word**.
3. Commandment Ten is in the sphere of **Thought**.

As God's law to Adam and Eve in the garden was both positive and negative. Positive - all the trees of the garden for food. Negative - the tree of good prohibited, so in the ten commandments there is both the positive and the negative.

Note however the positive is confined to the first table, and the second table are all negatives.

These Second Five place the emphasis on the sanctity of our neighbour while the First Five place the emphasis on the sanctity of God. The First Five list our duty to God. The Second Five list our duty to man.

THE SANCTITY OF OUR NEIGHBOUR

1.   Commandment Six - The Sanctity of our Neighbour's Person:-*'Thou shalt not kill'* Exodus 20:13.

2.   Commandment Seven - The Sanctity of our Neighbour's Purity:-*'Thou shalt not commit adultery'* Exodus 20:14.

3.   Commandment Eight - The Sanctity of our Neighbour's Property:-*"Thou shalt not steal'* Exodus 20:15.

4.   Commandment Nine - The Sanctity of our Neighbour's Position:-*'Thou shalt not bear false witness against thy neighbour'* Exodus 20:16.

5.   Commandment Ten - The Sanctity of our Neighbour's Place:-*'Thou shalt not covet thy neighbour's house, thou shalt not covet thy neighbour's wife, nor his manservant, nor his maidservant, nor his ox, nor his ass, nor anything that is thy neighbour's.'* Exodus 20:17.

THE SIXTH COMMANDMENT
'Thou shalt not kill' Exodus 20:13

Here we have the sanctity of our neighbour's life. By the way, our Lord defined who our neighbour is, in His parable of what is known as the Good Samaritan (Luke 10:25-37).

Life is the most precious thing. Its unlawful destruction is the most heinous of crimes and God demands a life for a life, for murder is a strike at God Himself. The murder weapon raised against the creature is a murder weapon raised against his creator.

God made a law which as long as man was upon this earth was never to be repealed.

'But flesh with the life thereof, which is the blood thereof, shall ye not eat. And surely your blood of your lives I will require; at the hand of every beast will I require it, and at the hand of man; at the hand of every man's brother will I require the life of man. Whoso sheddeth man's blood, by man shall his blood be shed: for in the image of God made he man.' Genesis 9:4-6.

Thomas Watson aptly said:-

'Though this commandment, 'Thou shalt not kill' forbids private persons to shed the blood of another, unless in their own defence, yet such as are in office must punish public offenders, yea with death if they sin. To kill an offender is not murder, it is but justice.

A private person sins, if he draws the sword; a public person sins if he puts up the sword. A magistrate ought not to let the sword of justice rust in its scabbard. As magistrates should not let the sword be too sharp by severity so neither should the edge of it be blunted too much by leniency.'

Alas today our Province and the United Kingdom are drenched in innocent blood - the victims of terrorism and the massacres of innocent babes murdered by abortion in their mother's womb. The sword of justice rusts in the government's scabbard.

It is our duty to preserve our own lives and the lives of our neighbours. Remember, *'Whosoever hateth his brother is a murderer: and ye know that no murderer hath eternal life abiding in him'* I John 3:5.

Remember also, *'Hereby perceive we the love of God because he laid down his life for us; and we ought to lay down our lives for the brethren'* I John 3:16.

All those sins which lead to murder we must continually guard against, such as envy, hatred and unjustified anger.

These sins are the vanguard to murder itself.

1.   Murder can be committed by our hand as Joab. We must guard our hand (2 Samuel 20).
2.   Murder can be committed by the mind. We must guard our mind (I John 3:15).
3.   Murder can be committed by the tongue, as the Jews. We must guard our tongue (John 18:30).
4.   Murder can be committed by the pen, as David (2 Samuel 12:9). We must guard our pen.
5.   Murder can be committed by planning, as Jezebel (I Kings 21:10). We must guard our planning.
6.   Murder can be committed by poisoning. We must guard our poisons.
7.   Murder can be committed by intention, as Herod (Matthew 2:8 and 13). We must guard our intentions.
8.   Murder can be committed by designing, as Saul (I Samuel 18:17). We must guard our designs.
9.   Murder can be committed by consenting, as Saul of Tarsus (Acts 22:20). We must guard our consents.
10.   Murder can be committed by our not preventing, as Pilate (John 18:38). We must guard our preventive powers.

11.   Murder can be committed by our unmercifulness, as the man who takes away the sustenance of life (Deuteronomy 24:6). We must guard our mercy.

12.   Murder can be committed by our leniency, as the judge who should have sentenced the murderer on his first murder but let him off, thus enabling him to commit more murders. We must guard our leniency.

Murder is capital crime. We should take capital steps from committing it. What an awful sin the Christ rejector is constantly committing.

'He that despised Moses' law died without mercy under two or three witnesses:

Of how much sorer punishment, suppose ye, shall he be thought worthy, who hath trodden underfoot the Son of God, and hath counted the blood of the covenant, wherewith he was sanctified, an unholy thing, and hath done despite unto the Spirit of grace?

For we know him that hath said, Vengeance belongeth unto me, I will recompense, saith the Lord. And again, The Lord shall judge his people.

It is a fearful thing to fall into the hands of the living God.' Hebrews 10:28-31

Killing the Prince of Life! Murdering the Son of God!

THOU SHALT NOT KILL!

THE SEVENTH COMMANDMENT
'Thou shalt not commit adultery' Exodus 20:14

Here we have the sanctity of our neighbour's purity.

'The fear of the Lord is clean, enduring forever.' Psalm 19:9.

This commandment demands that we preserve our own purity by preserving the purity of our neighbour.

Adultery wrecks our chastity on the rocks of uncleanness. Sex outside marriage is condemned by God.

The marriage is divinely instituted and sacred. God has hedged it around with a great prohibition and with great penalties. Those who break this hedge will be bitten by the serpent (Ecc. 10:8). Love and faithfulness are the great sustaining pillars of marriage.

Marriage resembles the mystical union between Christ and His church.

Adultery is a dishonour to God. It is deliberate. It can be prevented (I Cor. 7:2).

1.   It is the worst sort of thievish sin. It is the stealing of his neighbour's own flesh. Marriage makes man and woman one flesh. (Genesis 2:24).
2.   It is beastly in nature (Jer. 5:8).
3.   It pollutes the whole person (Luke 11:24).
4.   It is destructive of the body (Prov. 5:11).
5.   It robs men of their substance (Prov. 6:26).
6.   It everlastingly blots the name (Prov. 6:32,33).
7.   It is heart breaking (Hosea 4:11).
8.   It brings swift judgment (Deut. 20:10).
9.   It damns in hell (I Cor. 6:9).
10.   It endangers the soul of another.
11.   It is abhorred of God (Prov.22:14).

Thomas Watson states: *'The adulterer is the devil's first born, he is unclean, he is a moving quagmire, he is all over ulcerated with sin. His eyes sparkle with lust, he is so filthy that if he die in his sin all the flames of hell will never purge away his uncleanness.*

And as for the adulteress, who can paint her black enough: the scripture calls her a 'deep ditch'. She is a common sewer, whereas a believer's body is a living temple. The body of a harlot is a walking dung hill.'

To be kept from the sin of adultery we must:

1.   Keep ourselves from the whorish man or woman (Prov. 5:8).
2.   Make a covenant with our eyes (Job 31:1).
3.   Dress modestly (Prov. 7:10).
4.   Take heed of evil company (Psalm 106:18).
5.   Turn away our eyes from beholding vanity. Immoral films, plays, pictures and books (Ps. 119:37).
6.   Mind our eating habits. Gluttony and drunkenness are the vanguard of uncleanness (I Cor. 9:27).
7.   Beware of idleness (2 Samuel 11:4).
8.   Honour our marriage relations (Ezek. 16:49).

'It is not having a wife, but loving his wife which makes a man live chastely.'

Thomas Watson remarked that *'some have concluded because the Bible says 'none that go to her (the adultress) return again' that adultery was the unpardonable sin'.*

Not so. The meaning is, that 'none of those who keep going to her return again' (Ecc. 7:24).

David was delivered and restored and wrote scripture in his recovered joy of God's salvation.

Mary Magdelene whose eyes were wanton with lust, washed the Lord's feet with her tears from those very eyes. There is forgiveness with God. But, nevertheless, this is the most fearful of sins.

Our souls however, can have recourse to the precious cleansing blood of Christ and to that fountain opened to the house of David - remember he was an adulterer - and to Jerusalem - remember it was a city which became a harlot Isaiah 1:21 - for sin and for uncleanness (Zech. 1:21). Listen to these Gospel words:- *'Come now, and let us reason together, saith the Lord: though your sins be as scarlet, they shall be as white as snow; though they be red like crimson, they shall be as wool.'* Isaiah 1:18.

THOU SHALT NOT COMMIT ADULTERY!

THE EIGHTH COMMANDMENT
'Thou shalt not steal' Exodus 20:15

Here is the sanctity of our neighbour's property.

If God's holiness rightly demands we should not commit adultery then God's justice rightly demands we should not commit stealing.

A man can commit robbery either because of need, or because of greed. Robbery in both cases flows from unbelief in God and covetousness - a desire for getting.

If we truly believe in God, no matter how low our circumstances, God will provide for us.

'I have been young, and now am old; yet have I not seen the righteous forsaken, nor his seed begging bread.' Psalm 37:25

An immoderate desire for getting, that is covetousness.

As Thomas Watson said, *'A man covets more than his own, and this itch of covetousness makes him scratch what he can from another.'*

Stealing is the brat of the devil. Satan entered into Judas and Judas became a thief (John 12:6).

It was the sin of theft to which Satan hired Eve. To rob God of what was His property alone, the fruit of the tree of the knowledge of good and evil.

Eve and Adam both robbed God. That was the sin which brought all other sin into the world.

At the beginning of the history of the old economy the sin of stealing was seen, and so at the beginning of the history of the new economy the sin of stealing was manifested when another man and woman, Ananias and Sapphira, robbed God.

1. There is public stealing, like the thieves on the Jericho road (Luke 10:30).

2. There is concealed stealing, like Micah (Judges 17:2) who stole from his mother.

3. There is prevaricating stealing when the law is twisted to justify the robbery, as Micah discovered when his own thieving chickens came home to roost (Judges 18:19,25).

4. There is church stealing, robbing God of His own as Ananias (Acts 5:3), refusing to pay God's tithe.

5. There is business stealing, false sale prices, false weights, false measures and false guarantees (Prov. 11:1).

6. There is money-lending stealing, the stealing of extortion (Neh. 5:7).

7. There is trustee stealing. The trustee who robs the widow and orphan and becomes false to his stewardship and trust (Neh. 5:5).

8. There is borrowing stealing. The borrower who has no intention of paying back is a thief (2 Kings 4:7).

9. There is stealing by receiving stolen goods like Gehazi (I Kings 5:26). Such a receiver is a godfather of thieves.

Property has to be protected. God has set this hedge of divine commandment about man's property.

The remedy for stealing is obedience to God's Word by the grace of God.

'Let him that stole, steal no more but rather let him labour, working with his hands the thing which is good that he may have to give to him that needeth' Ephesians 4:28.

God can bless the little meal in the barrel. God can increase the little oil in the cruise.

'Let your conversation be without covetousness; and be ye content with such things as ye have: for he hath said, I will never leave thee, nor forsake thee.' Hebrews 13:5.

THOU SHALT NOT STEAL!

THE NINTH COMMANDMENT
'Thou shalt not bear false witness against thy neighbour'
Exodus 20:11

The sanctity of our neighbour's position.

The tongue which takes God's name in vain will not be slack in taking his neighbour's name in vain. The tongue is an evil weapon. James tells us, *'Even so the tongue is a little member, and boasteth great things. Behold, how great a matter a little fire kindleth!*

And the tongue is a fire, a world of iniquity: so is the tongue among our members, that it defileth the whole body, and setteth on fire the course of nature; and it is set on fire of hell.

For every kind of beasts, and of birds, and of serpents, and of things in the sea, is tamed, and hath been tamed of mankind:

But the tongue can no man tame; it is an unruly evil, full of deadly poison' James 3:5-8.

The evil tongue seeks to destroy the position of the target of attack. Undermining the character and credibility of the object of its vile calumny is the aim of false witnessing.

When that evil tongue, ablaze with the fire of hell, enters upon an operation of false witnessing, what terrible results the victim will suffer.

False witnessing has destroyed homes, families, marriages, businesses, churches, societies, prospects, thrones, governments and nations.

False witnessing inflicts three deadly wounds:-

First, a deadly wound upon the victim. How many victims have been so fatally wounded by the poisoned dart that they were never able to recover? Their character was so undermined that their future could not be saved nor their present position salvaged. The slander has left the finest of positions and the best of characters in ruins.

Secondly, a deadly wound to the one who told of the slander. The lie sown in the mind brings forth a deadly harvest. Doubts and verdicts contrary to truth result. The wound has been made and in the majority of cases is fatal.

Thirdly, a deadly wound in the soul of the slanderer himself. He wounds himself by wounding others by falsehoods. Slander is a sharp two-edged sword. It is a boomerang of hell.

You can kill an individual as well in his name as in his person. There are those who would not steal a man's goods but think nothing of stealing his good name.

This is a wound they cannot bind up. This is a blot which cannot be erased. God Almighty will not hold the false witness guiltless.

False witnessing can be engaged in against a person. It can also be used in the interests of a person. Both are lying operations.

When it is made, aided by perjury, the sin is then greatly aggravated.

No wonder the Bible tells us that all liars shall have their part in the lake which burneth with fire and brimstone. (Revelation 21:8).

We need the Divine sentinel to be always on duty at the door of our lips so that we break not this solemn ninth commandment of God.

'Set a watch, O Lord, before my mouth; keep the door of my lips.

Incline not my heart to any evil thing, to practise wicked works with men that work iniquity: and let me not eat of their dainties.' Psalm 141:3-4.

'If any man offend not in word, the same is a perfect man and able to bridle the whole body' James 3:2.

THOU SHALT NOT BEAR FALSE WITNESS AGAINST THY NEIGH-BOUR!

THE TENTH COMMANDMENT

'Thou shalt not covet thy neighbour's house, thou shalt not covet thy neighbour's wife, nor his manservant, nor his maidservant, nor his ox, nor his ass, nor anything that is thy neighbour's' Exodus 20:17.

Lastly we have the sanctity of our neighbour's place.

Notice the order. The neighbour's house comes first. This is changed by the Church of Rome and made second on the list. The house here is of course the home.

How precious is the home, that's our own place. It is the most precious possession we have on earth.

Covetousness is an insatiable desire of getting what we lust after.

1.   Covetousness is manifested in worldly thoughts.
2.   Covetousness is manifested in the amount of time spent seeking worldly things.
3.   Covetousness is manifested in the conversation totally dominated by the world.
4.   Covetousness is manifested in the heart being set on worldly things.
5.   Covetousness is manifested in the man being over loaded with worldly affairs.

6.   Covetousness is manifested in the man seeking by any means to achieve his lusts.

It is a deceitful sin, for the Bible tells us it is a cloaked sin (I Thess. 2:5).

It is a dangerous sin, the bitter enemy of grace (Matt. 13:7).

It is a deadly sin, for the love of money is the root from which there is a deadly fruit and that fruit is, all evil (I Timothy 6:10).

Covetousness breaches every one of the nine other commandments.

Covet not thy neighbour's home. It is his holiest of all.

Covet not thy neighbour's wife. She is his greatest treasure.

Covet not thy neighbour's servants. Seek not to tempt them away from their master.

Covet not thy neighbour's animals. Be like Samuel and be able with him to say:

'Behold, here I am: witness against me before the Lord, and before his anointed: whose ox have I taken? or whose ass have I taken? or whom have I defrauded? whom have I oppressed? or of whose hand have I received any bribe to blind mine eyes therewith? and I will restore it you.' I Samuel 12:3

Covet nothing of thy neighbour's. Be like Paul:

'I have coveted no man's silver, or gold, or apparel.' Acts 20:33.

Covetousness locks the door of heaven against you.

'For this ye know, that no whoremonger, nor unclean person, nor covetous man, who is an idolater, hath any inheritance in the kingdom of Christ and of God.' Ephesians 5:5.

You cannot get through the door to heaven without parting with your covetousness.

1. Faith will rid you of your covetousness. I John 5:4. *'This is the victory which overcometh the world, even our faith.'*

2. A right mind will rid you of your covetousness. Galations 3:2, *'This only would I learn of you, Received ye the Spirit by the works of the law, or by the hearing of faith?'*

3. Coveting earnestly the best gifts will rid you of your sinful covetousness. I Corinthians 12:31, *'But covet earnestly the best gifts: and yet shew I unto you a more excellent way.'*

Covet heaven, Covet love, Covet spiritual power, Covet blessing, Covet the presence of God, Covet Christ.

These ten commandments are the words of God.

Therefore:-
Receive them
Reverence them
Remember them
Rely on them
Respect them
Repeat them
Be Ruled by them

ROME'S GREATEST INDICTMENT

Spurn that Antichrist system of Rome which makes them all of none effect by its traditions.

1.   Rome makes the first commandment of none effect by having a whole series of beings, including Mary, lined up for worship along with God.

2.   Rome makes the second commandment of none effect by explaining it away and then eliminating it altogether.

3.   Rome makes the third commandment of none effect by taking God's name and transferring it to the popes in awful profanity.

4.   Rome makes the fourth commandment of none effect by hijacking the Lord's Holy Day as a Holiday and placing other days on a plane of equality with it.

5.   Rome makes the fifth commandment of none effect by transferring the honour due to parents to the pope and his priests.

6.   Rome makes the sixth commandment of none effect by being drunk with the blood of the martyrs of Jesus Christ.

7.   Rome makes the seventh commandment of none effect by allowing the sin of fornication and adultery, by giving both patents and pardons for all sorts of sexual uncleanness and by declaring when adultery is not adultery in God's eyes.

8.   Rome makes the eighth commandment of none effect by making stealing in certain circumstances null and void.

9.   Rome makes the ninth commandment of none effect by dispensing with oaths and lies at will, even at times holding lying to be lawful.

10. Rome makes the tenth commandment of none effect by practising the most highly organised system of covetousness the world has ever seen,

plundering homes, destroying lives and appropriating money, lands and property at will.

'*Thus have ye made the commandment of God of none effect by your tradition*' Matthew 15:6.

Weigh Rome, Antichrist Rome, in these Divine balances of God's standards and she is found, before God and men, wanting.

The Ten Commandments of God are Rome's greatest indictment. She stands totally, irrecoverably and eternally condemned.

Let none of us be like her, found in violation of the Only Word which can save us and make us live forever.

6 Precious and glorious
views of Christ

An exposition of the different views of Christ in the Bible. This sermon was preached in Martyrs Memorial Church in 1972.

IF YOU HAVE YOUR Bible or Testament with you, I wonder would you open it with me at this first chapter of John's gospel. The trouble with God's people today is this, that they simply skim over the Word of God instead of digging into one particular verse or a few of the great verses of the book.

They think that there is something that will merit them blessing if they take vast chunks of scripture. I believe that the art we have lost in the church today is the art of meditation. We do not meditate upon the Word. When you open any book of the Bible its opening words are important, and they are worthy of consideration. For sometimes we discover that in the opening words of a book we have a golden key which opens the whole book for us.

OPENING WORDS OF JOHN'S GOSPEL

Now let us look at the opening words of John's gospel chapter one: "In the beginning was the Word." You never read those words without thinking of Genesis chapter one.

Turn over to the first verse of the Bible, you will find it is: "In the beginning God." So the Spirit of God is drawing our attention to an interesting parallel between the first part of Genesis and the first part of the first chapter of John's gospel.

You're all familiar, aren't you, with the fact that Genesis chapter one and Genesis chapter two record seven days? Now if you would look closely for a moment with me at John's gospel chapter one and John's gospel chapter two you will find there are seven days.

I would like to draw your attention to this very interesting parallel. If you look with me at verse twenty-nine it says "the next day," so the day before that was the **first** day. That was the day when John said: "I am not the Christ. That was the first day. In the first day of John's gospel chapter one, John said: "I am not the Christ".

In the **second** day he said "Behold the Lamb of God".

Then look at this verse thirty-five: "Again the next day after." There is the **third** day.

Then look at verse forty-three, "The day following that is the **fourth** day.

Note the third day, chapter two and verse one: "And the third day". That is the third day from that fourth day. If you read it carefully you'll find that is what he book says. And that is **seven** days. If you would sit down some time and put the first day of John's gospel chapter one with the first day of Genesis chapter one and go down the seven days you will find there a most unique and interesting parallel. I'm sure you would get something for your soul if you would study it out with the open Book before you.

THREE VIEWS OF CHRIST

This afternoon I want to speak to you about three views of Christ which you have in John's gospel chapter one. First of all you have an **eternal** view of Christ in verses one, two, three and four.

In verse fourteen we have a **time** view of Christ. He's coming into time: "And the Word became flesh."

In the last verse of the chapter you have the **future** view of Christ. "Verily, verily, I say unto you Hereafter." We're in eternity now. Hereafter means after here, it's not hard to know what it means. After this old world is done, we're going to see heaven opened, and the angels of God ascending and descending upon the Son of man.

So we have an **eternal** view of Christ. We have a **time** view of Christ and we have a **future** view of Christ .

CHRIST IN ETERNITY

Now when you look at the eternal view of Christ, you'll find that there are seven views here, bringing out seven wonderful beauties; seven wonderful characteristics; seven wonderful things about our wonderful Lord.

First of all, when you read the first verse it says: "In the beginning was the Word" or "In the beginning the Word was already." Jesus Christ had no beginning, Jesus Christ will not have any ending. We had a beginning but praise God we have been lifted and we have been put into the eternal Christ, so we'll never have an end. We had a Genesis but we are never going to have a consummation.

Ten thousand billion years from today we'll be in the courts of the everlasting temple of heaven, and we'll be praising God with songs so beautiful that if we could have sung them down here we would have been the greatest singers in the world.

What a day that's going to be! Brother John and I are going to sing an eternal duet up there in heaven.

There were preachers who sang a duet one day in prison and there was an earthquake. No wonder! I never heard preachers singing in harmony yet. Praise God there's going to be a day of blessing.

"In the beginning the Word was already."

There is His tremendous eternity. I'm glad today that my Saviour is the eternal Christ. Get that into your heart and you'll face this year in victory. Our Christ is not a Christ that can be cast down by the ravages of time. Our Christ is not a Christ who gets weary. The End, the one Who is the Beginning, and the one Who is the ending, the one Who is the first and the last, the eternal Creator, He never grows weary.

We get weary. Humanity is bowed down with its own weariness. This old world is stamped and has upon it the seal of its weariness. But Jesus Christ faints not, neither is weary.

He is the eternal Christ.

Go out tonight and look up at the starry heavens and remember before there was a heaven for he stars to move in, away out yonder in the milky way of God's eternity there was a bright and morning star. Go out and look at the beautiful garden with its flowers, but remember before there was a garden in earth, in the garden of heaven there bloomed the eternal rose of Sharon. Remember my friend He's the eternal Christ.

He'll look after us, He'll get us through. There'll be heartaches and head-aches, and troubles and trials and difficulties and afflictions and misrepresenta-tions in the incoming year, but best of all Jesus will be the same.

Friends will let us down, people we trusted in will break our hearts, we will carry the remains of loved ones to the tomb, but praise God Jesus will never die. He's the Christ that lives. Get this into your heart today. This is what we need as we go on in life, to know He's the eternal Christ. "In the beginning the Word already was." This is a tremendous eternity.

CHRIST'S SPECIAL IDENTITY

Then I want you to notice His special identity, He's called the Word three times in that first verse. Look at it: the Word, the Word, the Word. You know words have a threefold significance.

First of all you can't communicate what you have in your mind except you use words.

You only know what I'm thinking when I speak. You might pretend to read my mind but you could not do it. There are no such things as mind-readers, although I know there are people who profess to do it. That is only a lot of baloney, they can't do it. But how do I set out my mind? I express it by words. Do I know the mind of God today?

Do I know what the great omnipotent, omniscient Jehovah's thinking? Hallelujah! Because Christ is the communication of the Father's mind. If you want to know what's in God's mind from all eternity, look at Christ.

The Lord Jesus Christ is the head of the church. What was God thinking about from all eternity? About you and me in the church. He thought about us before the hills in order stood or earth received her frame. Away yonder in the eternal ages of the past God the Father thought about me, Hallelujah!

I'll get through no matter how many popes roar in Rome. I'll get through. No matter how many devils roar in hell at us we'll get through all right. You don't need to worry, because the Word is the communication of the mind. What is God thinking? Look at Jesus.

I'll tell you something more, the Word is the representation of the per-son. I had a couple of poor souls got married today, and when they came into the room afterwards they had to sign their names. When they signed their names on the marriage register book they were a representation of their persons. That represented them. When you get a cheque and take it to the bank, you have got to put your name on the back of it, haven't you, to endorse it? Your signature represents you. Jesus Christ is the Word because Jesus Christ is God's representative to me. God is veiled in mystery. I don't know whether you've ever thought about the intricate eye that an angel must have. I wonder have you ever thought about the being of an angel. The angel dare not look on God, but with two of his wings he covers his feet, and with two he covers his face, and veiled with his own wings he cries, "Holy, holy holy".

God is shrouded in mystery. How can I reach Him, He's above me, how can I understand Him, He's far beyond my ken. Praise God I touch God in Jesus Christ, He's bone of my bone, He's flesh of my flesh, I can see Him, I can handle Him, He's the Lord of Glory.

This is what John was talking about in the first chapter of his epistle. Look at it, I John 1: "That which was from the beginning, which we have heard, which we have seen with our eyes, which we have looked upon, and our hands have handled, of the Word of life;" Hebrews chapter one: "God, Who at sundry times and in divers manners spake in time past unto the fathers by the prophets, Hath in these last days spoken unto us by His Son."

That's the representative of the person. The Word is something more.

The Word is the revelation of the heart.

It is not only the communication of the mind, and the representation of the person, but it is the revelation of the heart. That night, friend, that you took out the lady, who is now your wife , how did she know that you loved her? You plucked up courage to tell her. I know the sweat was sitting like beads on you, and your destiny was in her hand, and I don't know whether you even looked at her.

I am reminded of the story of a poor fellow who was in real trouble. He was in love with a girl and didn't know how to express it. So he got the hold of an old fellow who was married thirty years, and he said "Could you help me?" "Oh," he says, "I'll help you." He advised, "When you meet her tonight you say: When I look on your face time seems to stop," and then he said "get on with it".

So the fellow rhymed this over all day, and when he saw her coming at the appointed time and place he went up to her and he said, "Your face would stop the clock." He got a bit mixed up, didn't he?

But the word is the revelation of the heart. Do you know what's in the Father's heart? Look at Jesus. Look at Jesus. Do you know what's throbbing in the great Father-heart of Jehovah? Look at Christ, and you'll know how much He loves you. He loves you so much that he sacrificed His only Son for you. It seems to me He loved poor sinful men more than His Son, for He spared not His own Son, but delivered Him up for us all. A special identity, He's the Word.

The third thing about this is **His distinct individuality**. This is very important because there are people going about who deny the glorious doctrine of the Trinity. A friend of mine, who is a minister in Canada, told me that a Jehovah Witness came to his door one day, and when the pastor came out he said to him: "You're a preacher aren't you?" He replied, "I am." He said: "Explain the Trinity." He replied: "If I could do that it would be a quartet, it wouldn't be a trinity any more." The old Jehovah Witness left in confusion.

You can't explain the Trinity. Don't try to explain it, and don't let's try to bring this doctrine down to the puniness of man's little illustrations and representations. I don't understand the Trinity, but praise God I've met the Father, and I've met the Son and I've met the Holy Ghost.

I can't understand it, but I know that there is one God and not three Gods, and yet every person is distinct and every person is God. His distinct individuality: "He was with God". The word in the Greek brings out the meaning: "He was alongside God". That's pretty strong, isn't it? He's distinct.

The Father is not the Son, and the Son is not the Father, the Father is not the Holy Ghost and the Son isn't the Holy Ghost. And yet if you've seen Christ you've seen the Father, and when the Holy Ghost dwells in you He reveals the Son. Yes. He's distinct in His individuality.

He was with God. But that's not it all you know, look at the next part of it. His essential deity: "The Word was God". He was God, really was God. No mistake, no doubt here.

Isn't it refreshing to pick up the Bible after you hear these old rascals preaching on the radio. To pick up the Bible and find the Bible is firm on the Deity of Christ; the Bible is firm on the Virgin Birth of Christ; the Bible is clear on the miracles of Christ; The Bible is clear on the blood of Christ; on the resurrection of Christ and on the ascension of Christ; and, Hallelujah, on the coming again of Christ.

I thank God for the old Book. Isn't it refreshing to put the plugs in your ears and sit down with the Bible and say, "Praise God this is it, this is it." He's God without a question mark, He's God without limitation, He's God without boundary marks, He's God. You say, "Preacher, was he God when He was born?" Yes! I don't understand it, but praise God, I believe it. And when those men came from the East they didn't worship Mary or give Mary a present. No sir. They presented unto Him gold, and frankincense and myrrh, and it says "they worshipped Him". Yes. They didn't worship the creature, they worshipped the Creator. He's God over all, blest forever. This is Deity, His essential Deity.

Look at the next verse. I love this verse. **His personal immutability**, "the same". That's a great word isn't it? You should go through your Bible and you should mark all the texts about the Lord, that have to do with that word "the same."

It means He does not change. That means He hasn't changed in the past, it means He's not changing now, and glory to God He'll never change. He's "the same."

A little girl heard Chapman, the great American evangelist, preach. He was preaching on the second coming. The little lassie was terrified. She walked up to the preacher afterwards and she said: "Sir, I don't want Jesus to come." And he said "Do you love Jesus?" "Yes, I love Him." "Do you know him?" And the little girl said "Yes, I know Him." "Do you long to see Him?" "Yes, but I don't want Him to come. I was dead scared when you were preaching, you really frightened me the way you preached tonight I don't want Jesus to come."

The great preacher turned to the first chapter of Acts and he said "My little girl, wouldn't you like Jesus who came to Bethlehem to come?" "Oh yes sir, I'd love Him to come." "Wouldn't you like Jesus who lifted the children in His arms and blessed them, wouldn't you like Him to come? "Oh yes." "Wouldn't you like Jesus Who healed the leper, and gave sight to the blind and raised the dead to come?" "Oh yes I'd like Him to come."

And he said "My dear little girl the Bible says: 'This same Jesus' the same who helped you in the struggles of life, He's coming, He's the same, He doesn't change."

I'm sure you've had the experience, as every child of God has, of a sweet and blessed view of Christ somewhere along life's journey. There was a day when the sun really shone, you've had that experience haven't you? There wasn't a cloud between, and you walked with Him and you talked with Him and you told Him with the eternal voice of eternal thankfulness you were His forever. But as you went on in life the storm clouds came, and you've had your ups and downs. You've been down in the valley many a time and your view of Christ has not always been the same.

I want to tell you friend, that Jesus is the same. Do you remember that day He gave you a blessed view of Himself, well He's just as beautiful today as He was then. There may be something wrong down here but praise God there's nothing wrong up there, He's the same. I'm glad He's the same. I'm glad He doesn't change His mind. The Lord Jesus knew we were a pack of no-goods before He ever came looking for us. He didn't come to save saints, He came to save sinners, Hallelujah. He didn't come to save nice people, He came to save lost people. He knew all about you.

When He died upon the cross friend you weren't even born. But He knew all your life, and He knew how mean you would be and how twisted you would be, and how tough you would be and how unchristian you would be at times, He knew it all. He still loved you.

He knew there was a Jacob in every one of us, He knew there was an unlovely streak in us all, but praise God He loved us, and He's the same. He's the same.

Here's another great thing: **His absolute sovereignty**. "All things were made by him." That's evolution out altogether. You know we've got a lot of evangelicals, emphasis on the jelly for they're dead set, and they're trying to bring in the theory of theistic evolution. They say God was behind evolution. They're not just the old evolutionists, these are new ones. These ones have lost a little bit of the monkey's tail, they're not so horrid looking, and they call themselves theistic evolutionists. Listen friend, I want to tell you it's a lot of bunkum. God made man the way Genesis said He made him, and God made this earth in six days, of twenty-four hours each.

Yes, how do I know? Because God says, "Remember the Sabbath day to keep it holy, six days shalt thou labour and do all thy work." And if they were days as some of the evangelicals make out, of thousands of years expanse, then we would never get to the Sabbath. But praise God they were six days, twenty-four hours each, yes, just the ordinary days.

We've got all the "smart alecs" you know in the churches today. They like to take apart this old book. Friends believe this book, that's all you need do, just believe the Bible. Don't try and get any fancy interpretations to square up with some old bald-headed unbeliever, to make him think that you're with it. Oh let me tell you friend, He made all things. Well if that's true He made the devil, and I'm glad God knows the machinery of the old devil, He made him. He can put him out of gear just at the right time, He knows how to put the devil out of action.

And he even made the Pope, the Antichrist, yes, and he can put him out of gear too. And He made every old ungodly infidel that curses this church, and every old hireling prophet, wolves in sheep's clothing, that mounts the pulpit. My, Christ made them all. He can deal with them. Yes, every circumstance he can deal with, every trouble He can deal with, every sickness Hallelujah, He can deal with. Yes he can deal with these things. "All things were made by Him, and without Him was not anything made that was made." Yes evolution is out. That blows the monkey up so high you couldn't find even a tip of its tail when it comes down. It's all destroyed.

And there's something else. Look at verse four and we've only got these seven views of the Christ of eternity. "In Him was life." His life is unique vitality. In Him was life. All life is centred in Christ. All life.

See that little bird whichflies, Christ gave him life to fly. The beasts of the field owe their life to Christ. The very breath that's in the old devil, was Christ that gave it to him.

But I want to tell you something more. There's not only natural life, and angelic life, and the life of Satan. I want to tell you something, thank God, there's spiritual life in Christ: "He that hath the Son hath life." And if you've got Jesus you've got life, life that will carry you to heaven.

You know water will always rise to its source, and praise God the life of God within us will take us some day from this old earth and will put us on the throne of His glory.

Life, life, abundant life, Jesus alone is the giver. Seven views of Christ.

CHRIST IN TIME

The eternal Christ. Look at the Christ in time. A time view of Christ. "And the Word was made flesh."
His wondrous humility
The Word was made flesh. The invisible God took upon Himself the form of man. Here's a statement in the book, only the Holy Ghost dare write it, "He was made in the likeness of sinful flesh" made in our likeness sin apart. He was without sin. And He couldn't sin. Jesus Christ was not able to sin. There's a difference between saying that and saying he was able not to sin. He was not able to sin. He's the impeccable Christ. Some of these "wise alecs" come along, they tell us today that Jesus Christ was able not to sin but He could have sinned. A

principal in the Irish Baptist College is trotting out that nonsense. But I want to tell you that my Saviour was not able to sin. There is a great difference. The Word was made flesh. Yes. He came. What did it mean for Him to come from the Throne? There was no room for Him at the inn, His virgin mother is about to deliver Him and the old inn-keeper says "Get away, I've no room for you."

And the world has still no room for Jesus. And Joseph said, "We'll better just go and shelter among the cattle and asses." And there amidst the beasts of the field in a lowly cattle shed my Saviour was born. His mother had no little cot to lay Him in. Before our children came my good wife had the little cot already prepared, and the sheets and the pillow ready there, and the little blankets made with mammy's careful hands.

But Christ's virgin mother had a long, weary journey, no nice cot for Jesus, no little blankets, no sweet soft pillow for Christ to lie upon. She wrapped Him in swaddling clothes, the very same clothes that He was wrapped in, in the tomb. She wrapped Him in a shroud, that's the meaning of the word, in the raiment of death, because He was born to die, that's why, and His birth was in order to His bleeding, and His cradling was in order to the Cross. His wondrous humility.

His glorious visibility.

This one rejoices our heart. "We beheld His glory." We saw Him. Oh I know there was a time when we looked on Christ and we didn't see any glory about Him. We passed Him by, didn't we?

What does the Bible say: "He was despised and rejected of men, a man of sorrows and acquainted with grief, and we hid as it were our faces from Him, He was despised and we esteemed Him not." We didn't care for Him.

Then one day the Spirit of God put eye-salve upon our eyes and our eyes were opened, and we saw Him. "His glory broke upon me when I saw Him from afar, He's fairer than the lily, brighter than the morning star. He's all my fancy pictured in its fairest dreams and more, and each day He grows still sweeter than he was the day before." "Ten thousand charms around Him shine, but best of all I know He's mine." We beheld His glory. And you know what happened to us. When we beheld that glory we were changed.

"But we all, with open face beholding as in a glass the glory of the Lord, are changed into the same image from glory to glory, even as by the Spirit of the Lord" II Corinthians 3:18.

May the Lord ever give us these glorious views of His dear self.